THE HAZARDS OF LOVE

STAN STANLEY

AN ONI PRESS PUBLICATION

AZARDS
LOVE

Writing, art, colors, and letters by **STAN STANLEY**

Designed by **SARAH ROCKWELL**

Edited by **HAZEL NEWLEVANT** and **AMANDA MEADOWS**

Assistant Editor **AMANDA VERNON**

onipress.com lionforge.com

snakewife.com /snakewifestanley

First Edition: March 2021

ISBN 978-1-62010-857-4

eISBN 978-1-62010-858-1

Printed in China.

Library of Congress Control Number: 2020937828

1 2 3 4 5 6 7 8 9 10

The Hazards Of Love Ø: An Honest Mistake

The HAZARDS of LOVE

OUR LADY
OF
MOUNT CARMEL
SCHOOL FOR GI

Hey.
Hey, Iolanthe.
Amparo?!
I heard you got suspended!

No, I talked to the principal.
I'm on probation.
Listen, I just wanted to tell you I'm sorry.
I'm going to be a better student.

I'm going to be a better person.

The previous day
BRM BRM BRM!
thumpathumpathumpa
SQUEAK
BRM BRM BRM!
=pant= =pant=
H-hey.
'scuse me.
READ
Is that the fire alarm?!
BRM BRM BRM! BRM BRM BRM!
BRM BRM BRM! BRM BRM-*
There's no fire, it's okay!
Just be cool.
I'm not cool!
I've never BEEN cool!

Respectfully, I beg to differ.
Quick, check the library!
Iolanthe!
Did you see anyone run past here?
I-I, uh, THINK so
it just all happened-so-fast!
Mm, probably hiding in the gym again.
Thank you, Iolanthe.
Mweh heh heh.
Ey, lemme know when it's safe to come out!
You can come out.

Whoa.
Maybe I'm better off down here.
Why would you do this?!
To me? To the library?!
You'll get in trouble! I'LL get in trouble!
=gasp=
I'm your
ACCOMPLICE.
Okay, you just made it sound super badass and awesome - but no.
If anyone gets in trouble, it'll be me and JUST me.
I didn't mean to make you freak out.
I just figured that while they're lookin' for me, we could... y'know, talk.
We don't really know each other, though. Why do you want to talk to me?
Uh, well, haha. Yeah, we uh. We don't really know each other that well, but I see you in homeroom, and.
Um.

You're cool, Iolanthe.
Is what I'm sayin'.
You're cool.

Nnnno?
I am the exact opposite of cool.
I love rules and also the library.

You're just doin' you!
That makes you the coolest girl in our class pretty much.
Is this some kind of trick?
Stop.
If you want me to do your homework, the answer is NO.

...Man, people have been real mean to you, huh.
wibble
Okay, look, I'll just - I'll tell you what I want.
If YOU want. Um. I wanna take you to the park after school.
And I wanna hang out with you and throw rocks at pigeons - or in the fountain, whatever doesn't make you mad.
And I'll buy you a hot dog and a soda and we'll sit under a tree and.
You know.
Just chill.

Oh.
I guess that's fine.
Cool.
Noooo, Io, you can't go out with AMPARO.
LADIES
We're just hanging out in the park!
Listen to me:
do NOT date a delinquent.
I-it's not a DATE!
Good.
YOUR HANDS
'cause Amparo's been suspended twice and you can SO do better.
IT'S NOT A DATE!
They said I was cool!
She also thinks shoplifting is cool.
Okay, but remember that my dad's had a "no lesbians in my home" rule after what happened with my mom.

HOT
Oh, God, this IS a date.

No. No, it ain't a date.
Not 'til you want it to be a date.
Then you tell me, "Amparo, this is a date."
And I'll say, "cool."
Then I'll be the happiest person on this planet.
Amparo...
I don't know if I, uh, swing in your general direction.
Okay but consider:
I am REALLY bad at being a girl and shouldn't count.
Oh gosh. I mean - or, I meant- So.
I care a LOT about school and, uh, grades, and.
And you have... other interests.
This is 'cause I got held back a year, huh.
N-no!
Well. Maybe a little.
But like, you knocked someone's head into a wall.
She called my mom a ugly
How could I NOT knock her ass out?
Amparo, you're funny, and I - I definitely don't NOT like you.
But.

But I don't know if I LIKE YOU like you.

I don't know.

I - I think I need to think.

Okay.

I'll see you at school, okay?

Sure, Iolanthe.

=snff=

=snff=

=snff=

=snf= Ah, [illegible] no.

Amparo?
WIPE
Did you pull the fire alarm at school today?
How can I tell your mother? She works so hard to afford a good school for you!
Why would you do this?!
I dunno.
You don't know. You don't know why you did it, don't know why you're getting suspended, don't know how to think of anyone but yourself!
Uh-huh.
That's all you have to say? "Uh-huh"?
Uh-huh.
Is that what you'll say to your mother?
When she gets home tonight with her feet aching from standing on them for hours?
...
Stay in your room and think about what you did.
I'll think about how to tell your mother.
One of us has to.

CLIC

That could have gone much better.

Amparo Uribe? Let me in.
The night is sweltering.

What.
You leave scraps of food on the fire escape for me.

Aw, damn, I thought I was gonna make friends with a raccoon!
...no..
Oh my God.
This some Jim Henson .

Hey, where's your battery?
Rude.
Now.
You seem to be in a bit of trouble!

Maybe. What's it to ya?
Me?
I had intended to repay your kindness!
But now I can see that I'm only troubling you.

I'll just be on my way, then, so sorry-
Whoa whoa.
Hang on!

Hanging.
You can't blame me for bein' suspicious a some Beyoncé-soundin' cat comes outta nowhere.
Also I'm havin' a bad day!
You saw.

Indeed. Well, how can I help?
Like a wish?
Ho am I getting a wish?!

Perhaps, if you word things correctly.
Make Iolanthe fall in love with me.

THAT'S what you'd wish for?
Can I wish for more wishes?
I should wish for more wishes.
Ugh.

What?
Those're good wishes.
They're selfish and manipulative.
You here to grant me a wish or be judgy?

KNOCK KNOCK
Amparo?

Hey, Mom.
Hi, amor.
Did Abue tell you...?
About the alarm? Yes.
But.
I can't fight about this now, Amparo.
Am I grounded?
It doesn't matter; you'd sneak out.
I need to sleep, vida, tomorrow is a double shift.
Good night. I love you.
Yeah.
Love you, too.
CLICK
A'ight.
I know what I'm wishing for.
Do tell!
Can you make me a better person?
Like.
Less stupid, better at school stuff.
Funny, maybe?

Hm. Well, let me take a look...
tm.
Yes.
Yes, I could improve your reputation!
With talkin' cat magics?
Yes, magic.
You'll need to sacrifice a bit for the magic to work!
I'll need a drop of your blood--
Do it!
OUCH!

There we are.
The !
So, uh.
Do you take tests for me?
Like Puss in Boots?
Don't be silly.
I AM you, now.
I don't think I'm really comfortable with this.
Oh, you shouldn't be comfortable.
I've just claimed your life.
What?
Your life. Your shape. Your name.
It all belongs to me, now.
You were supposed to help me.
Yes, that was a lie.
Lying is very easy.
You open your mouth, you make sound.
If you choose the right noises, people will do anything you want.

"Amparo Uribe."
I love it.
Like burnt sugar on my tongue. MY name.
No no no-
ABUELAAAAAA!!!
Oh, kitten.
She can't hear you.
You're less than a ghost!
There's no substance to you, silly!
I'm the real Amparo now.
A- A- Ah
Are you trying to say "Amparo Uribe"?
It's not your name anymore.
You've no right to it.

You can't do this, it's my LIFE.
There's no good in you, you know.
Oh? Had big plans for it, hm?
It's why I chose you.
More petty crimes here and there?
I'm going to apologize to my abuela.
If my mother is still awake, I'll promise her that I'll change.
Tomorrow, I'm going to turn my life around.
I'll cherish it the way you never could.
There's good in me.
Is there? Where has it been hiding?
A predator can use its words as well as its teeth.
My death?
When Bright World eats you.
Contemplate that, nameless creature, as you await your death.
Rustle Rustle

Aw,

I can't mess up again or they'll kick me out for good.

How'd you convince them to give you a second chance?

I was just honest, you know?

Put it all on the line.

So. Thanks.

You got me started on fixing what needs fixing.

I'm gonna make my mom proud of me.

I'm gonna have me a great life.

I might even get lucky enough to have a cool friend like you.

Wow.

You really do want to change.

After that wake-up call you gave me?

I'm an entirely different person.

The Hazards Of Love 1: Bright World

aaaaaaaaa
AAAAAAAAAAAAAAAAAAAAAAAAA
AAAAAAAAaaaaaa
shf
shf
SHF
SHF
SHF
SHF

=huff=
=huff=
WHOMP

...The ~~fuck~~ is that?!

=phew=
WIPE
HONK!

Move!
HONK! HONK-HONK-HONK-HONK!
Get out of the road!
MIMI
I'd be cool with that, but I kinda suck at walking right now.
'cause I'm INJURED.
Ugh, FINE, I'll move you to the side of the road.

I'm going to approach you!
You'd better not bite me!
=oof=
NUDGE
NUDGE
NUDGE
Hey, uh.
Insteada... this, could I get a ride to town?
Certainly not!
I JUST cleaned the car and LOOK at you!
Ha, yeah.
My ma would be makin' noise about infection-
My ma.
Okay, lady, lemme level with you.
I got scammed by a talking cat, thrown into this place, and now I'm tryin'a get back to Jackson Heights.
In the human world?
Yeah, in Queens.

Where's your license? You shouldn't be in Bright World without a license.
=sigh= The cat that scammed me didn't gimme a license, no.
Or a chance to put on shoes.
Ah.
Well, then, I really must be off; I wish wish you the best of luck.
WHAT!
Aw, no, c'mon, wait.
Sorry, but I really must be going.
You're just gonna leave me here?
I gently nudged you to the side of the road.
Back to the selva with you now, shoo.
Hang on!
Fff, I don't have my wallet-
As if I'd be seen touching human money!
I GOT GOLD!
MY EARRINGS ARE GOLD!
'S only a little, but it's real and good-.
And given to you by your grandmother!
Yeah.

I'll make you a deal.
The earrings for one ride to town.
Uh?
Fine, I'll throw in two suppers and three nights of boarding.
That should give you plenty of time to work out your license issues – I assume you will be going about that honestly.
Sure.
Get in, and don't bleed on the upholstery.
Yeah, okay.
You're so lucky I found you before anyone else, I've got a soft heart.
Thanks? Who're you?
Why, I'm
Mimí
Fifth generation of the revered a
and beloved S. Cuincle lineage, kn
entertainer, restaranteur, phila
hopeless urbanite, travel advent
trustworthy confidant, known
to be
a well
highly
coveted = and o
something of a
tastemaker,
obviously.
Jeez

Okay, well, I'll remember that. I'm...
...

!!!
GRAH.
???

...yes?
H-hang on.

ARG!
I KNOW THIS.
I KNOW MY NAME!
Are you cursed?

Sorta. It got stolen.
Oh. Well, that's not your name anymore, then, is it?
I guess not.
Don't worry, dear.

It doesn't make much of a difference either way.

Definitely not near Queens.

So, then, human.
You'll need to be at my home by Sky White hour.
I'm a respectable woman, you know, and I won't have people talking.
'Kay. You got an address?
824 Manto de Tisu. The station is a few streets away; you'll be done in no time.
Good luck!
...Huh.
273
Av. Man

TOP QUALITY "POLICE ASSISTANCE" HIGHLY RATED
Pretty worried that this is gonna suck for me.
SATISFAC
GUARAN
RIVATE
Ensure a Reputable Harvest
Please Ring Bell For Service

RING
RING
Hello, hello! Happy to serve, how can I help you?
Yep, hi.
You may have noticed I'm a human.
I'm tryin'a figure out my license issues and get back to my world.
What's wrong with your license?
That's what I wanna know!
It get lost in the mail or somethin'?
Hm, possibly.
Okay, but so you know, I'm pretty... DISSATISFIED.
Now, now! No need for the D-word! We'll fill out some forms and replace it for you!
I know you're just doin' your job.
But I gotta get to the human world ASAP. Once I'm there, I'll fill out the forms for you.
First priority is getting back to Queens, but if I gotta accept Brooklyn, I will.
...Wait.

ZZZZZIP
The Bright World residency specifically forbids travel to the human world by humans.
Well, obviously there's been a mix-up! I'll talk to my legal rep as soon as I get back to Queens.
Or Brooklyn.
I don't think we can do that, actually – oh!
Officer Ramón!
Can you help us out with this?
Sure, what's going on?
Human misinformed about transfers and permissions.
Oh, and a lost license.
Haha, so a lot of paperwork to file, huh?
Aw, well, I don't wanna be any trouble.
No trouble!
Let me get back there with you. Don Luis, can you get me an amended Form?
Sure, 12F or 12M?
Good question – sorry, are you a boy human or a girl human?
KNOW THE DIFFERENCE!
MINION
MORSEL
Greetings, superior!
polite, docile, aware of their place
glyph of sponsor
Where am I? What is this place?
confused, uninformed, panicked or upset
no glyph, no sponsor
DO NOT EAT!
YES, YOU CAN EAT!
I – wait, what?
Are you a boy human or girl human?
I am an INEDIBLE human.

I didn't know humans came in "inedible"!
Sorta. I'm edible, technically.
But only one bite.
I am THAT fuckin' poisonous.
Ooooooh.
...Unless someone's tryin'a use me as poison, then like, the person meant to be poisoned instead gets good luck.
Forever.
That's not useful at all! What form should we use?!
I don't know if we have a form for that - why would anyone bring in a human that's not edible?
Who's your sponsor again?
It's kinda complicated.
Shouldn't be. Should be refreshingly simple.
That's what I meant, it's so simple that it gets all complicated.
Are you familiar with well-respected and beloved community member Miss Mimí?
What?

Do you know who she is?
Of course!
I can't see her glyph on you, and she hasn't filed for another human as of late. So...?
Well.
That's where it gets complicated!
Hm Hm
Hmmm
Hmm Hm
Mm Hm Hmm
Hmm Hmm Hm
Miss Mimi?
Not now, Paola.
There was a message, though!
Your presence is needed at the police station immediately.
WHAT!

WHAT...
...seems to be the problem?
There she is! Miss Mimi!
Beautiful and kind even now.
Welcome! We've been told how brave and pretty you are!
Oh! Well, haha, my stellar reputation DOES often precede me! Haha.
WAG WAG
I do hope nothing is the matter.
The human has told us everything!

We heard you outwitted an entire herd of skullbeasts!
Nod nod
(whatever those are)
Blah blah, blah
Blah blah Blah blah Blah
Blah blah blah
Blah blah blah
Blah blah
Blah
And about how you drove away from a monster!
Blah blah
And then you generously offered to escort the pupal human into town so that they can sort their license issues legally!
of their place
Blah blah we just wanted to hand your human back and tell you how much we admire your bravery.
Officers... thank you.
However, I'm afraid you have it all wrong.

THE H
OF

I am no hero!
I'm a terribly shy person who hates drawing attention to my numerous kind and amazing deeds!
Ooh, she's humble!
I shall make all the proper arrangements!
But for now, I really must get home to steady my nerves.
It has been a DAY.
Bye, superiors.
Thanks for the water.
844
WHIRL
Please don't eat me.
I DON'T EVEN KNOW IF YOU'RE ORGANIC!!!

I'm not, I'm full of poison.
I can't BELIEVE you embarrassed me in front of such handsome men!
I didn't, though! They think you're nice.
I am ABSOLUTELY nice! I certainly don't need YOU vouching for my niceness!
No, but I gave 'em this story about how you're kind and generous.
Hmp!
And who knows what sorts of illegal activities you're going to try to implicate me in?
Aw fer 's sake, lady.
All I want is to get my ass HOME.
Well, that, and avoid getting ate, which is a thing that happens here apparently!
And yeah, I lied and said you were gonna be my sponsor–
Indeed!
–but I got one a the pamphlets to look through, and it ain't that hard! You don't gotta pay for me or nothin'!
I mean, there's like, a notary fee.
Uh.
But mostly you gotta sign some papers that say I'm an okay person.
Should you get a human?
A: Maybe.
ARE YOU GETTING A HUMAN
?
Why humans?
Edible!
Harvest!
Hard-Working!
PROS
CONS
Tempers!

Well, I don't know if you DESERVE it! I'm respectable!
And you. Are. CURSED.

You'll need a JOB! And somewhere to STAY!
Whoa, whoa.
You said I could stay with you for a few days!

I ABSOLUTELY did not! I said you'd be staying with my STAFF for THREE nights!
Okay, okay!
I will get on the job and housing situation SO fast, I swear!

Very well, human. I...
...shall TAKE A RISK.
Finally, thank you.
To my car!
Come!
Time will tell if you betray me or repay my kind heart.

Obviously, there will be rules while you are in my home.
I am to be addressed as MISS Mimi.
NEVER interrupt me while I am on the phone...

And don't even think of
=Sigh=
End of Issue 1

The Hazards Of Love 2: MiMi

-and absolutely no shoes inside my home.
Not gonna be a problem for me.
Good.

Choose a bed for yourself; you'll be sleeping here.

Good luck!
Thanks.
Hey.
...
Okay, y'all can be quiet if you want, I guess.
=sigh=
ow ow ow ow
Ow!
Hey.
There are socks and extra sleep clothes in the back cabinet.
Oh. Thanks.

So. You're in some trouble.
~~Shit~~, you don't say.
You're a person, yeah? Like me?
I'm human, if that's what you mean.
Yeah.
Hey, uh.
Does Mimi eat humans?
No.
Or kill us and sell our human meats?
She threatens to sell us to the butcher if we misbehave.
Does she?
Does it matter?
Go pick a cot and let me get some sleep.
Some of us have to work tomorrow.
Yeah... I gotta get a job, first.
You've been conned, you realize.
What?
No!
I'm the one doin' a con!
Are you, now?

Isn't this all a little convenient? How are you going to get a job with no license, no glyph, no phone of your own to get called back on?
...
Wait, they got phones here?
You hadn't even thought that far ahead.
Hey, I just got here!
Exactly.
You're struggling to stay one step ahead, and you need to plan ahead.
At the end, you'll have no job, no hope, and no time left. You'll ask for Mimi's help, and she'll generously offer a staff position.
That what happened to you?
I wouldn't know.
I don't remember.
Well. I'll get a job. Just you wait.
Good night.

The Job Search
~OR~ "Buscando Chamba"

HeLP Wanted
INQUIRE INSIDE
6+ limbs ONLY

LIMB EXCHANGE SERVICES
Reasonable Prices

Aw,

So, you don't have a real person's glyph on you.

I don't think so, but I got this, which means–

Which means you don't have a license.

Move along, sweetmeat.

Potential Resident
DO NOT EAT

Do you have much experience with beekeeping?

So. Very. Much.

EMPTY

Yes, I can certainly find a use for you at my bar - though you're woefully unskilled.
Still, I've taken one chance on you - what's another?
Uh-huh.
"Uh-huh." Listen to you!
The LEAST you could do is try to be respectful!
"Yes, Miss Mimi."
Or if I may be so bold...
"Thank you, Miss Mimi."
I don't want to be under any contract or nothin'.
Well, that's fair.
Frankly, I hope you find another job soon. But I will need to protect myself.
This clarifies how much you'll be paid per hour, plus the percent for commission.
Sign on the dotted line, please.
SLIDE
Name of Employee
...
Uh.
Can I just use an "X" or, like...?
Goodness, no; how very VULGAR.

You may use the communal name.
The communal name?
Why, yes.
Many humans sell their name, you know, to make ends meet, buy a little thing for vanity's sake, or just to have some pocket change!
You're hardly alone in being nameless. I'd never met anyone who lost their name before arriving here, granted.
So, what name do I sign?
"Paola."
I'll buzz someone to put you through orientation. You can start today.
So, all the others here – this happened to them, too?
Paola
You're an employee, dear! Most of the others here are charity cases, poor things.
They're more dead than alive; it's so sad.
I had to take them in, give them purpose, or I wouldn't be able to live with myself!
They're liable to stand in the same spot 'til their feet rot unless someone tells them to move.
Now, then!

Wait, how did they get that way?
I find it quite rude to discuss others' tragic personal circumstances, thank you very much!
Though I'll say they did seem to have a lack of passion.
SHFF SHF
I doubt you'll have that problem.
Here we are!
A uniform for you!
So you fell in her trap, huh?
Hey.
BZZZZZZ
Eat my actual ass, Paola.

Oh, I'm not a Paola yet. Juliana.
ZZZZZ
BZZZ
Good for you, I guess.
Your name is the last thing you sell off, it's that precious.
Yeah, I lost mine already.
So, you're pretty screwed, then!
Both me and you knew that already.
Start saving up for a new name.
Can't I just give myself a new one?
Not here in Bright World.
This damn place.
What even is it? Like, is it another dimension?
I haven't exactly had time to look into it.
Most people won't give you a straight answer.
They like keeping us in the dark.
So, what's the scam?
Indentured servitude.
Mimí pays just enough to keep you afloat on a good day. And on a bad day, well.
Expenses are subtracted from your commission.
So, make sure to sell enough to cover your room and meals.
What happens if you don't?
That's being in debt, stupid.

You can sell parts of your past or parts of memories to pay what you owe.
That what happened to the Paolas?
Yes.
Once you're scraped empty, Mimí doesn't have to pay you anymore, and you don't have the ability to fight for yourself.
So, she takes you in as a charity case and gets herself some free, brainless labor.
...Hey.
How long you been here for?
God.
Do you ever shut up?

What the do you got against me?!
I just told you.

You're the competition.

C'mon.
You're going to get dressed and learn how to sling drinks.
If you get out there not knowing how to do anything, we're both in for it.
Okay, but.
Can I get some shoes?

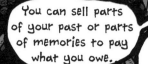

Damn.
The Paolas keep it all going, huh?
How many are there?
Five right now, but they wear out fast.
Unlike you and I, they're perfectly fine working 12-hour days with only a short break.
Well, "fine" is the wrong word.
Here, you can change behind this.
Mimi keeps them in the back where they clean and wash dishes.
My job - and yours, now - is to go out there and charm the money out of these chumps.
We'll do this democratically.
Half the room for you, half for me.
I'm still gonna need shoes, though.

=ulp!=

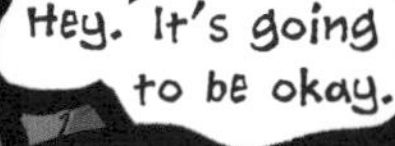

Hey. It's going to be okay.
Try to pretend they're regular humans who think we look delicious.
I'm serious. Be cautious, but not too cautious.
Here.
These have been in the Lost and Found for years now.

HEY
HEY
HEY!!!
TIME TO QUENCH YOUR THIRST!!!

Looking a bit slow there, sweetmeat!
Distracted by those pretty white teeth! Can barely focus on work!
Fancy a closer look?
Haha!
Maybe when y'all get the next round!
This drink is too monochrome.
Well, you went for the low price point.
Nothin' wrong with that, but you get whatchu pay for.
¿!! !! ¡!!! ¡¡!! !!¡¡¡! ¡!!!?
Yeah, bud! You deserve a nice sparkledrank! Get it!
UHR. WHAT CAN I GET FOR HALF A
One drink.
One.
Did you seriously flirt with Las Peludas?
Maybe.
I know they look like women, but they're not.
Haha, oh man, can I relate!
They see you as FOOD.
Then I better get extra spicy, make sure I look tasty as hell!
What does that even mean?
IT MEANS I CAN'T HEAR YOU OVER THE SOUND OF THE TIPS IN MY POCKETS.
CHKA CHKA CHKA CHKA

And after tallying up the register tonight, our top seller is Paola!
scribble
That's me?
Yes.
Awesome! I got this DOWN!
Now, I'll do some quick sums.
There's your base rate-per-hour, per ten hours, plus you get a 10% commission... the tidy sum of 1700!
Woo!
Now, subtracting the cost of your uniform...
Wait, what?
Just a starting cost, it won't happen again - unless you damage it and need another.
Kinda steep, don't you think?
It's a high-quality uniform!
That, plus the slippers and night shirt you took-
You're chargin' me for that?!
Do they just give clothing away where you're from?!
I'm trying to be fair, dear, and things do have a COST.
Now, what have you been eating?
Uh. Dust.
Hm, no, that's not right.
Aha! It says you checked in at the kitchen.
The chef noted you were "loud and belligerent."
=sigh= You know, dear, as long as you work here, you ARE representing me.
You could try to behave a bit better.

After all, I'll be vouching for you on the day you become officially licensed to reside here.
When you step outside, you wear a glyph that I have personally authorized.
I need to know that you are WORTHY of that honor!

Food for thought. Now, you've made...
...a total of 895 today.
WHAT!

Why, that TONE!
You could pay for your room and board for the rest of the week!
If I were you, I'd feel quite proud of myself!

ungrateful
NOW, on to Juliana.
Yes, Miss Mimí.
Lovely, lovely.
Let's do some math. Base rate, your usual commission...

Oh, but it seems you broke a glass?
Yes, Miss. Just one of the Barral Signatures.
No, no, that was Iztla.
What - but I thought-!
Oh, Juliana, what AM I going to do with you?
You're at a negative again, dear.
Do you have time left to sell?
Plenty!
A full week?
...
I have enough, Miss.
We'll schedule an appointment for you soon, then.
You're My *competition.*
GRARG FINE!

Yo, Miss! 'Scuse me, Miss!
Can I, like...
...cover my ass and transfer the rest to Juliana?
Oh! Are you sure?
Yeah, why the not, I guess.
SO NOBLE!
SHRUG
Juliana, you'll only owe me ONE day!
You should really be thanking your new friend!
Hey.
Hey.
Hey.

You're WELCOME.
You're so stupid.
There's no guarantee that you'll make enough money tomorrow.
You shouldn't have done that.
Even if you do stay afloat, there's the day after, and the day after that.
It never ends. You understand?
I understand. That's why we're leaving.
Heh!
I mean it! Let's go!
Great! Where are we going?
We'll figure it out along the way.
We just gotta get out now.

How fun!
We'll live on the streets!
Always paranoid!
Always at the mercy of the authorities!
Who do you think will get picked off by a predator first?
Me or you?
...
There's gotta be--
NO!
There is NOTHING! Nothing!
Three years. I've been here for three years.
I'm sorry to say there is nowhere to run away to, and I am exhausted from trying.
You think you're the first to come up with this? Really?
All we can do is work hard and hope that one day, we can get to the point where we can be a second-class citizen.
You know.
Instead of disposable.

Fine.
I'll find another way out.
Do it fast.
Do you know what it means?
When you owe Mimi time?
Yeah.
It gets taken from you, right?
Like off the end of your life?
You're certainly thinking like a Bright Worlder.
Some places here use time as currency, definitely, but here it's memories.
Your past. Days already lived.
They scrape them out of your brain and before you know it:
there you are, another Paola, nothing inside you.
Hence the desperation to find more things to trade.
Information, for one.
Tell me, how much is it worth to Mimi to know she's hired a traitor?
That they're planning on running away and sticking you with the bill?
You wouldn't.
Why not?

You don't know me. I don't want to do it.
But I have so little of my own left.
I have to be smart about what I sell off.
I try to keep important dates.
But there is so little of me left.
You'll understand when you're in a position like mine, if you last that long.
Sacrificing yourself for others isn't worth the risk here. It never works out.
I've learned that the hard way.

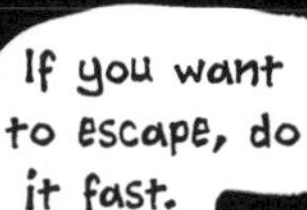
If you want to escape, do it fast.
You'll have from now until the day of my appointment for removal.

Good luck.
I'm almost rooting for you.

End of Issue 2

The Hazards Of Love : Hands And Feet

Hey.
This is dumb, huh?
Yeah.

Oh! Uh, no offense.
Haha, it's okay.
None of this was my idea, I'm just set-up.

I blew up half the balloons before I figured out we had a balloon pump.
That was less than awesome.
Ha!

How's probation going, aside from the grunt work?
One month down, three to go. I'm doing okay, though!

Ohhh, I LOVE this song!!!
It's a good song!
...d'you wanna dance?

You don't have to.
No.

But I think it might be fun.

You saved the dance from being awkward!

It's still kind of awkward.

Also my mom gave me a WINK, and I cannot deal with that.

Heh, yep. Sorry.
Still, you were gr-
SMECK
Yeah.
Uh.
It was nice seeing you!
...
... Bye.
Bye.

Ey.

Eyy,
Amparo.

Where you
goin'?

HSSSS!

HOLY

What do we do?
We can head 'em off--
No.
Let 'em go.
What?
That ain't them.
Dolorosa
Mom? I have kind of a weird question for you.
Okay!
Let's hear it, amor.
Can a person undergo a sudden, major shift in personality without intense trauma?

At your age? Yes.
Something going on?
Someone I know changed their entire personality in, like, a month.
Is this Pritha?
Because her parents' divorce has been hard on her, and-
No, not her.
But that is a good example.
If you were her doctor, would you tell the school what was going on?
If she asked me to, or if it was something very, very serious.
It helps educators know why someone might need a little space.
Or maybe why they have a shorter temper than usual.
Mhm, mhm.
Would a thing like that be in their file at school?
Maybe. I can't imagine that would be available to the public, though.
MmHM.
DETENTION NOTICE
Student: Iolanthe Luz Marquez Grade: 10
Date of Incident: 04/29 Location: Library
Reason for Detention: Abuse of library privileges, Attempting to "hack" school computers.
Corrective Action: (First offence) Meeting of counseling with Principal Miller, restricted access to school computers.
Administrator Signature
Date
Hand this to Mrs. B when they call you in.
Okay.

Hey.
Didn't know you had it in you.
That's not them, y'know.
What?
"Them."
Amparo wasn't a girl.
Oh. I knew that!
That thing look like Amparo, but it don't FIGHT like Amparo.
Th-they said they wouldn't be fighting anymore.

That's different.
I mean they INSTINCT.
How feet move, how you think, am I gonna run or am I gonna fight.
That ain't Amparo.

My mimi was from the island, and she'd say a evil spirit got in 'em, like a ghost.
People say you kissed them at the dance.
But you ain't dumb. You know something about them is wrong, yeah?
...
My gramma's Catholic, and she'd say Amparo got the Devil in 'em and you need to run a fresh egg on they body while praying Our Father.

Jamila Everly.
Or maybe they a vampire now.
I dunno.
But I don't trust them.

You shouldn't, either.
Dolores
Huh.

Okay.
Okay.

feliz Cumpleaños
I just gotta pick the right one.

Doooon't mind me, just topping you off, my guy!
Noticed you were runnin' low there.
SPLISH
But I gotchu, man.
Just keep it between us.
Also if you need, like, a butler or a chef or, uh, anything...
Thank you for the drink.
OKAY, but I'm a creative problem-solver, and I run real fast and can fix a
Thank you.
For the drink.

So much for that cheap...!
Workin' on the same drink since he got here.
WHO?!
Who refuses to buy our beautifully made drinks?
Guy in the corner chair. Antlers.
Oh.
Him.
No darling, he's much worse than a cheapskate.
He's a man with self-control.
He's reasonably well off, but refuses to indulge in vice. Why even have wealth, then?
Right?!
If I was loaded, I'd buy a whole bathtub full'a sparkledrank.
Don't waste your energy on silly fantasies - or on him.
shove
He'll nurse that one drink all night.
In fact, don't even speak to him.

You again?
Me again.

Do I need to speak to Mimi about this?

I'ma leave you alone. But first, I'ma level with you.
I'm in a real bad place here.

I'm workin' hard.

But Mimi charges us for the air we breathe, chips away at us. I stay here, I may as well be dead.

So yeah, I'm lookin' for a way out.

This place is loud as hell. Makes it hard to read that book, huh?

Perhaps I'm here to socialize.

Then you're doin' a job, 'cause since I went on the clock, you been here in this chair and you ain't said a thing to anyone.

I mean.

Let's be real, I'd do the same if I could.

And there's that birthday party over there.
Keep lookin' at you.
Waitin' for you to get up so they can steal this plush chair.
Feliz Cumple
Mm.
I could make you this same drink at home.
Or the friendly ambience.
So, what, you here on business?
Tell me.
Be your personal chef and bartender. Maid? Butler?
I didn't come to this place for the drinks.
Why are you speaking to me?
What specifically made you pick me to try this on?

Why not the farmer instead?
...
Because he's loud and big and he drinks hard and yesterday he could barely cover his tab.
I don't know.
Then go bother him.
And here I am, quietly reading my book.
Mimi said you don't like to buy booze, right?
I control my drinking, yes.
So you're less likely to scrape out my insides for money.
I could outright eat you.
Fuck, at least I'd die quick.
You don't know.
Fine, I'll back off.
Enjoy your drink.
Your feet as fast as your mouth?

Like a bullet from a gun.

Mm. I'm not going to pay anything you owe Mimi.

Why you think I been bustin' my ass all night?

I got nothing I owe her. So I'm good to go.

Good.

Well, let her know you'll be going, then.

Really? Just like that?

Well. Let's pretend you lied to me about your skills.

How long do you think I will take to find out?

Not long.

And what do you think will happen to you then?

Something bad?

I knew you looked clever. Let Miss Mimi know.

I'M FREE, YOU ANCIENT HAG!

FIRST of all... HOW DARE you?!
Less "dare" and more "deer," turns out!
As in... I'm runnin' away.
With the deer guy.
What?
YEAH!
I told you not to speak to him.
Mimi.
El Ciervo!
I'd like to have a brief word.

Hey!
I'll need to reschedule our appointment.
Incidentally, I am taking this one.
No!
Yes.
Go get your things. We're leaving.
I got nothing to go get.
Disgraceful.
Ahahaha, er.
Sir, sir, there's just... so much more fire to this one than the others!
So, you can exploit her, you mean?
Them.
So you can exploit them, you mean?
Sir, please, I just – it's so busy these days, I just need an extra pair of hands!

Well, then.
Hey!

Why didn't you say so?

GRAB

What're you-

SHUNK.

The Hazards Of Love 4: Al Mal Tiempo, Buena Cara

And how DID you end up in Bright World?

Well. So, like. This talking cat promised to help me out, right?

And instead it stole my name and my shape and shoved my ass in here, and now it's livin' my life.

Ah, I see.

A talking cat that you'd known for a long time and whose betrayal was impossible to see coming.

Look, in my world – ah, s–sorry.

Take your time.

In–in my world, we got, like, this fairy tale

And the stories tell you about talking animals that give yo free wishes and help you out.

That's what I thought was happening.

You had well–documented precedent, then.

Indisputable facts.

Look, if you wanna call me stupid, just do it. I get it.

I'm not calling you stupid.

But you've made stupid decisions.

I point this out so you won't repeat your mistakes.

I shoulda known better.
That shit happens to pretty white girls and not...
...not brown whatever-the-fuck-I-am...s?
Whatevers-the-fuck-I-am?
How do I make that from one to more'n one?
You're fading. Here, drink some water.
The cat got all judgy, too, like, "Oh, you're a bad person. Oh, you don't deserve a life or a name." And like...
Fuck you, cat, you don't know me, you don't know my life! You try walkin' where I gotta walk.
Mm.
Then you tell me if you don't learn to beat the shit outta everyone who's tryin'a beat the shit outta YOU.
You're going to drink this slowly.
Hrrrgbrble wrble
What? No. Shut up and drink.
HRR GRBLE HKK COFF COFF=
Oh, honestly.
"Not dying" doesn't seem to be your strong suit.
Haha, you'd be surprised!
HKK coff=

Sorry.
PAT PAT
It’s alright, it could’ve been much worse.
Hey. I ain’t stayin’ in Bright World.
Mm?
I’m gonna go back home.
Maybe I’ll beat up a cat, I dunno.
Did we not just talk about the bad choices you’ve made?
I’m just warnin’ you. Like, I’ll pay you what I owe you, but I’m gonna get my name back and go home.
My mom’s livin’ with an evil cat!
So far, it seems like the only danger is that the cat may treat her better than you did.
Ouch, but...
No.
She’s a talkin’ cat with magics.
Think there’s more danger there than just my wounded pride or whatever.
...
’ A, how long’re we gonna walk?
Awhile.
Parking is hard to find.

If I were you, I'd put the idea of returning to your world out of your mind.
Yeah, uh, nah.
Nah, that ain't happening.
Suit yourself. But you won't be returning.
There's no way for you to get from here to there.
I ain't buyin' that. The cat did it.
Yes, it's a cat.
Obviously it did.
Although I am surprised it wasn't eaten.
You may not have noticed, but humans and cats are very different.
I NOTICED!
What about you, could you go?
In general, Bright Worldians don't. Your world doesn't care for us and the feeling is mutual.
Those of us who enjoy humans are satisfied with the ones who wander in.
So, you're gonna eat me, huh?
Well, I don't know, it's a long drive.
I may get hungry.

'Kay, but you prolly shouldn't, 'cause. I'm poisonous.
Are you?
Yeah!
One bite and BAM, you die!
I see.
We're playing that fun game where you tell me a blatant lie and then I tell you a blatant lie.
My turn, is it?
I'm so glad you decided to insult my intelligence.
I'm not poisonous.
You're not poisonous.
I'm very familiar with humans.
I'm a physician, you know.
Oh, yeah?
Yes. I was almost a butcher, in fact, but at the end of the day, I prefer them alive to dead.
Cool, cool, that's good for me. I want to not be dead.
That's the spirit.
Can you get into the car on your own?
Uh, actually, I could really use a hand.
Or two, if I gotta be honest.
Mm. I don't care for puns.

Well, I guess I'm feelin' kinda contrary.
Are you?
That'll certainly take you far in life.
CLICK
YOU CUT OFF MY HANDS!
And raising your voice to me will not get them back.
Honestly.
You're fine.
You're not losing any more blood.
I feel sick.
That's shock.
If you pass out, I will eat you.
Stay conscious and pay attention.
I'm payin' attention.
I'm payin' attention.

Leave your shoes by the door.
'Kay.
Nice place.
Thank you.

Remember, you're not a charity case.
You're here to do a job.
We'll start with simple cleaning.
If you do adequately, I'll file the paperwork to formally employ you and ensure your survival.
Uh-huh, uh-huh.
So.
I'm down with it, but I wanna make sure you remember this one lil' THING.
I got no hands.
Yes, I'm aware of that.
I was the one who cut them off.

Oh, good. Good. We're on the same page 'bout how that went.
So, uh, it's gonna be a challenge to clean around here...
WITHOUT ANY HANDS.
Like. You get that, right?!
You get that?
Aren't you a creative problem solver?
Did you lie to me?
Did you lie about your ability to work here?
I'll be fine.
Oh, good.
Let's get you situated.

Do you prefer trousers or a dress?
Huh? Oh.
Trousers usually, I guess.
But I'll take whatever I can pull on easiest.
...
SHFF
'Cause a my havin' no hands.
Yes, I gathered.
Let's start you with a simple shift.
To keep things easy.
...And so I don't have to look at that hideous thing you've got on.
I'm down with that.
You can burn this dress, if you want.
I will HELP.
Mm.
So, just to clarify for me.
You are currently without a name.
...Yeah.
I mean.
If you wanna get technical.

Let's address that when you're done being an eyesore.
'Kay.
Ah, good, you're finished.
So.
I've decided you will answer to "Fawn."
That's simple enough for you to remember, yes?
'Course.
Well, let's practice.
Hello, Fawn.
Hey.

...Thanks.
Mm?
For the name.
Ah.
Well, don't try selling it or anything like that. The name is for my convenience, not yours.
Yeah.
That's pretty obvious.
Do I need, like, a license so I can go outside and not get eaten? I had this bracelet from Mimi-
You'll need a sign that you have a patron in Bright World, yes.
But you don't need to worry about that just yet.
See if you can earn your hands first.
You'll be a bit limited for awhile.

For real, though.
I dunno that I make a good "Fawn."
Like, you think a "Fawn," you think a someone all girly and fragile and delicate.
White. Blond, prolly, with big eyes and like, she's always cryin' or somethin'.

But whatever, that's me, that's my name now.
shff
And here I am, cleaning this damn house.
Since I'm all up close and personal with it, I've noticed something.
There are all these empty shelves.
SSSSSS
Nothin' on 'em.

All these empty photo frames.
No photos.
Shrines full a plain white candles, but no saints or nothin'.
PSSSSHH
Just empty.

I dunno how so many plants live in Bright World.
Ain't no sun.
Ain't no moon.
There's kinda this night and day, though.
The sky's either ink black or white, like salt.
At Sky White, the neon colors settle down, go all muted and pale.
Or El Ciervo does, anyway.
He don't talk much.
He got me pads when I bled, and he cut my hair when it got all long.
El Ciervo sleeps when the light goes all soft and milky, so I think Sky White is their night?
And Sky Dark seems to be when most people work.
So, I guess it ain't all bad, 's what I'm saying.
Except he does sneak up on me real quiet when he needs something, and it scares the hell out of me.

He makes coffee for us in the mornings when the sky is graying. It's less him bein' nice and more him makin' sure I know how to do it right.
He gets me food to eat, at least.
I've never seen him eat, though, not once.

Which makes me like, 200% sure he's a vampire or, like, some kinda bloodsucking monster that eats humans or feeds on souls or memories or love or something.

He drinks his coffee, reads his newspaper...
SLURP
...and I try to eat breakfast without hands, 'cause they got cut off.

I can't really read the writing they use down here, but the pictures are okay.

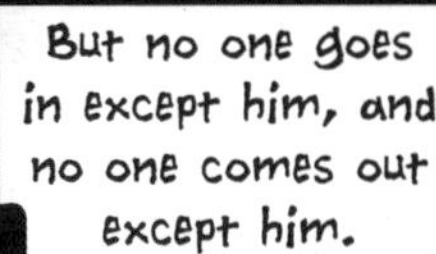

When he's done, he goes to work, which means he locks himself in his office for hours.
I'm not allowed to go in there, so I don't know what he does.
He says he's a doctor, so prolly he's cutting up people or doin' experiments or some like that.

But no one goes in except him, and no one comes out except him.

Except... then there was today. Things changed.
And today was weird for a lot of reasons, but mostly...
...I realized I been here for almost two months.
That's a long time for a evil cat to be living with my mom and, and, and...
Sorry. I got distracted.
Why didn't you interrupt me?
Well, Fawn-
Hey, uh, you don't gotta call me that.
Ohhhh, but of course I do, Fawn!
I could NEVER ignore such an obvious tie to your patron, El Ciervo!

Should I even be suspected of disrespecting you by, say,
treating you as my equal,
(Or interrupting your very fascinating and not at all boring monologue,)
El Ciervo will visit and carve the skin off my limbs!
I wish that was a joke.
Haha, me, too!
I'm so stupid.
I thought he was my best bet.
You did fine. There's no such thing as a best be in Bright World.
You did fine.

If you'd gone with the blue capybara, he'd have you working the field in his stead, and then he'd just drink away any money you made for him.
You could've done worse when it came to it, I mean.
Okay, but.
El Ciervo did very much cut off my hands.
Let's... let's not forget that part.
And by the way, if you see 'em anywhere around here-
They were fried up for a birthday party that same night.
Oh, boo-hoo!
You don't seem like you'll be missing them!
You'd be surprised.
These really ain't the same.
END

The Hazards Of Love 5 : Idle Hands

Let's see what you can do with a little more freedom, hm?
They're not really solid?
You have to make them solid.
ffffSSSSSSSS
Motherf-
Don't be petulant or I'll take them away.
SSSS
GLM

You've worked without hands for weeks now.
These simply require practice.

...so. This ain't a complaint or nothin', but...
...why now?
To be perfectly honest...

...I'm tired of opening the door for you all the time.

Valid, but I ain't buyin' that.
Clever. Follow me, then.

So, I can have, like, knife hands?
Yes.
I'll be sending you to market to pick up some things for me.
If anyone attempts to disrespect me by slighting you, I want you to eviscerate them.
This is an order.
=sigh=
I'm sorry, you're a child.
At least TRY to eviscerate them.
Just do your best.
Okay, but,
I'ma be sixteen soon.
So, not a child.
Sixteen.
Well, that's eviscerating age.

"Al Mercado"
Bag containing: crumbly tablets (currency?)
Featuring:
- New hands!
- New name!
- New outfit!
Map of this area
Actual pants
Handkerchief (for nose-blowing)
Shoes that fit!
There we are. Now.
Feel free to explore if you're feeling brave or particularly good at not getting lost.
Just be back and have your chores done by Sky White.
Aren't you gonna give me a glyph or a permission slip or something?
Mm? No, you're clearly my property. You'll be fine.
Um.
Y'sure this'll keep me from gettin' ate?
Let's find out.
CLIK
Ey!!!

MERCADO GUSTAVO
ARREGLOS FUNERARIOS
Y MUCHO MUCHO MAS

Ey. I need some service here.
Well, hello, morsel-
Nuh-nuh-nuh. None a this "morsel" stuff.
I'm here shoppin' on behalf of...
...El Ciervo.

Yeah, you know that name, huh.
Ha, of course!
I'll be right out with his order.
Hell yeah.
AHORA
Jugos "Marcos"
Hey.

I'm here to pick up some oranges for El Ciervo.
Really.
Is that so?
en venta todo electronico
Are you human?
I like to think so.
You tell me, kiddo.

...Do I look human enough?
I dunno, man, might be a Bright Worldian wearin' a human skinsuit or somethin'.
Heh.
'S weird here.
It is.
And hey, it doesn't hurt to be cautious here.
But I'm 100% human, I promise.
... Okay.
Who do you work for, then?
No one. See a glyph on me?
No.
But, like, I don't got one on me either.

YOU don't need one.
Those hands are a dead giveaway.
They announce him even before you open your mouth.
I'm Rafael.
I'm Fawn. But you prolly knew that.
Listen, Fawn, I'm gonna tell you the most important thing you need to know here:
Humans here have to stick together.
No one wants to end up in his bad books.
Well, word got around.
Our chances to scrape some information together.
It increases our chances of survival.
You don't have to trust me right now.
But don't wait too long.
You're with El Ciervo. You're going to need all the kindness you can get.

Here. The oranges are his, the juice is for you.

Come back another time.
I'll tell you what little I know.
EN

KNOCK KNOCK
Hey...
You in there?
I went to the market and no one asked me for money, and they all seemed to know what you want, sooo.
That's a thing.

CHK CHK

CHK CHK

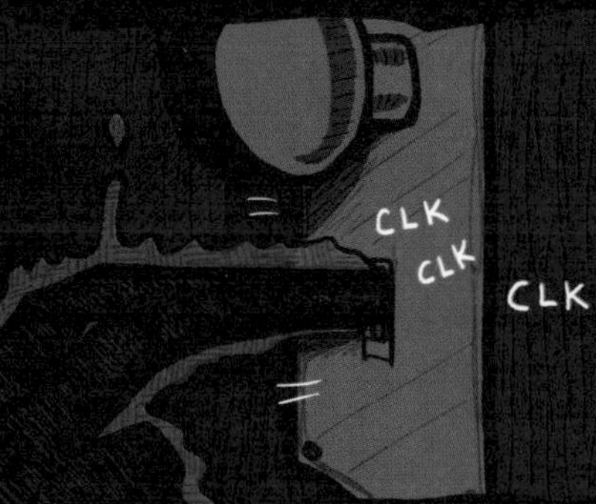
CLK
CLK
CLK
Oh, hey, looks like you left the door open.
CLK CLK CLK CLK
And you weren't answering, so I tried the door. And here we are, me in this unlocked room.

. . .
There's gotta be some evil hiding here.
No WAY this is just an office.
No diagrams a dead bodies.
No drawings of brains or guts or whatever.
...Is this in Spanish?
Yes.

Human writing is much easier for taking notes, you understand.
I see you survived the market mostly intact.
You seem to have returned with an unasked-for disregard for privacy, however.
Y-you didn't answer-
And you took the initiative.
Let's analyze this, shall we?

This is not the time to lie to me.
You picked the lock.
You used your hands?
Yeah.
Why? Curiosity?
I guess.
Y-you weren't answering-
the door was open-
You're not doing particularly well at controlling yourself.
shRug
Look at this.
Hey!!!
You're so excited to have hands again that it's spread up your arms.
So unbecoming, Fawn.
Look, I was just bein' nosy, okay?!
Sorry!
You disappear all day, I - I wanted to know what you do.

Do you think you made a mistake?
What?
Would you say you made a mistake?
ANSWER.
OW!
Yeah, it was a mistake!
's sake!
You think I'd wanna set off the who cut off my hands?!
NO!
An excellent point.
The problem, Fawn, seems to be that you have trouble understanding that your actions bring about consequences.
The fault lies with human developmental neurobiology.
Your brain has yet to develop what it needs for you to make rational decisions.
Let's give it some help.

What-
no!

No! No!
Nooo!!!

Oh.

Yes.

Oh,

Aren't you
the erudite.

Here, I'll help you down.
Where ARE we?
Is all that blood mine?
Not anymore.
Come along.
Where's the door?
No, no door.
Wh?
How.
Mm.
I may teach you one day.
It's a skill.
Now.
Your body and mind have been through a lot.
I'm giving you the rest of the evening off.
Likely you're feeling disoriented.
Sit, try to relax. You need to heal.
I'll bring you some juice.
What the ?

By the way, you're missing something.
A large fragment of memory is carved out.
From its size and shape, likely attached to an object you had on you - jewelry, perhaps. A watch?
Something to think about, at any rate.
So yeah, it was a weird day.
It's awful, isn't it?
The way he feels in your mind. Like an icicle.

...Yeah. Well.
That's why I'm here. I need-
You're here because Mimi hired him to scrape out the last of a Paola.

...Okay, that too. But while he's busy, I'm tryin'a figure out what I'm missing and who has it.

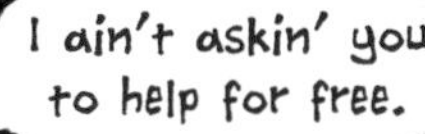

I ain't askin' you to help for free.

Pft, good.
But I AM askin' you to help me.

(...This IS currency, right?)
Yeah!
Since when do YOU have money?

I had some left over from no one taking my money at the market.
You in?

Well. I'd at least like to know what you had in mind.

I got an idea.

End of Issue 5

The Hazards Of Love 6: Belling the Cat

THN!!
Fine.
He's doing a full scrape, so it'll take him roughly double this timer to finish.
Keep an eye on the sand. You do NOT want him to hear us.
Now.
What do you want to know?
Gimme a sec, there's a lot to figure out!

What. WHAT.
What you mean, "what"?
Why are you giving me that LOOK?

You should kno
JAY!
SLAM!

What is?
Uh.
Look behind you.

VOTE FOR PROM!
MONARCH
QUEEN
Amparo Uribe
Iolanthe Marquez
=sigh=
IOLANTHE!!!
Oh no, not now.
I have been looking ALL OVER for you!
We are going to have a CHAT.
Pritha-to-Iolanthe!
You IGNORED me in Lit when we paired up so you could work with AMPARO.
...Fair.
Ha!
Now that I think about it, you're the first to leave and come back here.
=coff=
What else did you want to know?
(You gonna yell at her, too?)
Jay, sh.

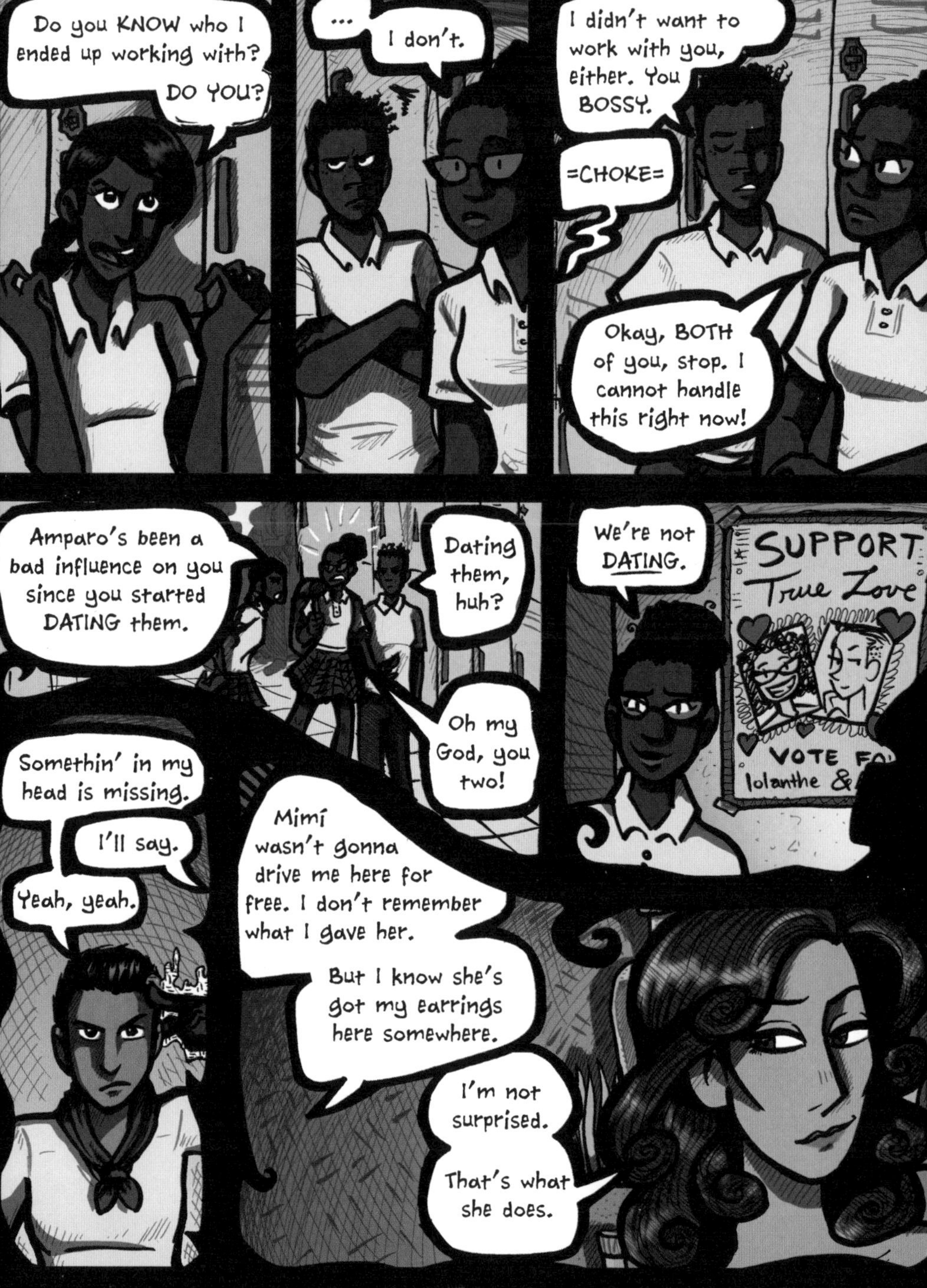
Do you KNOW who I ended up working with?
DO YOU?
...
I don't.
I didn't want to work with you, either. You BOSSY.
=CHOKE=
Okay, BOTH of you, stop. I cannot handle this right now!
Amparo's been a bad influence on you since you started DATING them.
Dating them, huh?
We're not DATING.
SUPPORT True Love
VOTE FO
Iolanthe &
Oh my God, you two!
Somethin' in my head is missing.
I'll say.
Yeah, yeah.
Mimi wasn't gonna drive me here for free. I don't remember what I gave her.
But I know she's got my earrings here somewhere.
I'm not surprised.
That's what she does.

If you're not dating, then what's with the ad campaign?
Yeah.
I honestly have no clue.
VOT
No matter what, the popular girls will NOT let this happen, okay?
No way.
Ohhhh, Iolanthe...!
Today, I am God's punching bag.
WE have a proposal for you!
It's been my job for awhile now. The Paolas aren't very good at critical reasoning, so they can't be trusted to do it right.
Ohhh, that's right.
Mimi didn't think you were competent enough to clean her boudoir.
There are dozens of little boxes, each with a small piece of jewelry inside.
She calls them her nest egg.

We will be permitting you and Amparo to win prom queen and monarch.
Obviously not because you've worked for it.
But because the St. Francis boys need to be punished for their crimes!
What crimes?
Ignoring my texts
Thinking I'm easy
Asking Toni and me for nudes on the same day
Unacceptable fuckboyness in general.
What better way to pull the rug out from under them than to prove we don't need them for our prom king?
We'll have a prom queen and a prom monarch – BOTH from our school!
So, like, a memory gets attached to an object, right?
But Mimi also gets El Ciervo to scrape people's brains out.
Yes.
So, that means two things:
One: for whatever reason, she can't scrape us out on her own, or she would've cleaned us all out soon as she could.
And two: El Ciervo can do that shit, no problem.
I'd even guess he enjoys doing it.

It'll draw media attention, look good on everyone's college applications...
Including yours.

You're a good candidate, given that you are the prettiest of our school's sapphically inclined types.
H-how did you know?
HAHAHAHAHA HAHAHAHAHA
Iolanthe.♡

He's so creepy.
Haha, yeah.
Even the other Bright Worlders are afraid of him. Whatever he is, he's not like them.
They can't carve through minds like he does.
How come HIS house ain't full a jewelry?
I have a theory.
I think he does something else with the things he removes.

Hello, motht beautiful.♡
Come down, Amparo.
We need to have a chat.
Did you see the posters?
Yeeeah.
I think he makes these out of us.
Our lives, our memories, condensed into a little tablet.
Ffff and they use it as money?!
And the kicker?
SHKASHK SHKASH
It's just a different way to consume us.

But you've seen the posters.
Yes.
Aren't they cool?
I bought them.
With money.
Money from my job.
Amparo.
man.
You're supposed to ask me before you do something like this!
Before I buy posters?
They use coins, too, and they'll exchange objects that have memories attached to them.
I think it's just another thing to use in bartering, y'know?
The hell even IS their economy?
Heh.
It's all a bit abstract.
FLIP

You never asked if I wanted to be Prom Queen!
Oh.
Why wouldn't you?

Some of it is contradictory. Some of it makes no sense at all.
We don't know their rules, and they won't tell us.
For all we know, this could all be a game to them.
And meanwhile El Ciervo mines us for our memories.
He can do more than that.
He can take your ability to smile.
Your sense of humor.
Your literal heart.
Damn, how does anyone survive that?

Well, they do their best to live productive lives.
Never love again, I suppose.
No one survives that, Fawn. Humans die without their literal heart.

That's not the point!
Why didn't you ask me first?
Are you angry?
Yes!
That doesn't make sense, though.
Makes perfect sense to me!
No, I mean...
I have perfect hair. I'm succeeding at school. I have a part-time job. I have a girlfriend I kiss a lot.
Who wouldn't want to be my prom queen?
Is that why you kiss me?
Am I just a bullet on your list of things you're "supposed" to accomplish?

Did you ever actually like me, Amparo? Or did you just like the idea of having me?
I-
Iolanthe!

=WIPE=

I'll be prom queen. That decision was made for me, and I can't fight it. But after that, we'll graduate.

And I won't hang out with you again.

Nah, look.

Like. Where's Mimi now?

Her office.

But she keeps her bedroom locked up!

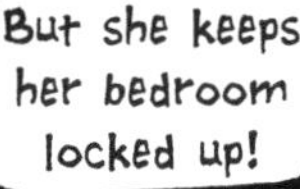

Bet I can break in.

And then what, you'll rummage?

Nope. You'll have told me which a them is my box.

You're asking for a lot.

I might just betray you, instead.

MAY 15 FRIDAY

MAY 16 SATURDAY

J. Everly and Pritha Mukherjee!
What an occasion! The first at our school!
Better luck next year, St. Francis fellas!
Okay, FINE.
=ulp=
I won't betray you UNLESS I'm backed into a corner.
But here's how it's going to go.
One: you pay me. I'm really stickin' my neck out for you.
I need to be able to take care of myself, y'know?
Yeah.
Two: you NEVER mention getting me out of Bright World ever again.
But-
Yes or no, Fawn.

No shame in crying, Kyle!
This wasn't easy to change up all last minute.
Let's hear it for the happy couple!
But I worked my magic.
Took advantage of the corrupt prom voting system.
Managed my best.
Yes.
...
Stay calm.
Grab my hair.
And kiss me hard.

I've been so anxious.
I know. I'm sorry I hurt you.
Do you understand why it hurt me?
No. I'm still sorry, though.
=sigh=
I love you.
I love you so much.
SLAP
AAAH!!!
The next time you try that, I'll remove the hand that struck them.

I've tried to change, to not be awful-

Stop.

I hate it when you do this, I hate when you act like the old you was evil or something.
No.

You were reckless, you were irresponsible, but you were a KID, you know? You've grown up, you've changed!
Stop beating up the old you.
I loved them.
I... I love you.

You.
I leave you alone for an hour, and you waste your time flirting with THIS?

Yeah, I was bored and she's cute.

Haha, I had all these plans for my life.
But now I'm just so scared
that you won't keep me.
Please keep me.
Please.
Amparo.
AAA!
That's my fault, I suppose.
Next time, I'll bring something for you to READ.
nng
hkk
nnnn

Fawn.

We're leaving.

Yeah.

End Of Issue 6

The Hazards Of Love 7 :: Si fuera falso

Sure, I'll help you out.
...
You don't even know what I'm askin' for.
Don't have to.
You came to me for help.
I'll do what I can.
Well?
Spit it out, kid, I don't got all day.
I need you to pick out my groceries.
Just this week and next.
I'll pay you and everything, I just, uh, need you to have 'em ready when I come back in a few hours.
...Yeah.
Yeah, okay, I can do that.
You feel like sharing what you're doing with that free time?

I'm gonna get my memory back.
Good.
Who's got it?
Yanno, for a guy who's all, like, "human solidarity," you ask a lotta questions and don't give a lot back.
Heh.
So, ask me.
!
Well, what's your deal?
I'm Rafael Loya.
I don't know how long I've been here, exactly.
I've had to sell a memory or two, but I've still got all my flesh on me.
And I'm gonna find a way out.

Ha, you too, huh? We're in the same boat.
You find anything out so far?
Yeah.
They make the rules and change them as they please.
I got more to share, but time's wastin'.
Scram, kid.
"You taking the bus?"
"Yeah."
"Take some oranges for the musicians.
"They get annoyed if you don't tip."
BRRRRMCHCHCHCH
Supli
Supli
Mi Reina

Next stop, Calle de la Republica.

MiMi's
JINGLE
Hey.

SNAP
Thanks, Paola.
15 mins
(Bed)
Under vanity
"Disposing of this message is going to be difficult.
"But first, send the Paola back inside or she'll just stay there."
Uh.
You should go back now.
Probably.
"Rip this note into four pieces. No more, no less.
"Bury one immediately, right here, right now.
"Throw one into a flowing river after you cross.
"Burn the last piece and make sure to eat the ashes.
"When you're halfway home, throw one piece into the breeze and let the wind take it."

So, this is how I woke up today.
My hands quit leaking.
I see.
I can still shape 'em, but does it... mean anything?
It means you'll start keeping my calendar.
Nah, but for real.
You'll use ink.
Your penmanship will be perfect.
Don't make me a liar, Fawn. I'll be awfully hurt.
And then so will you.
Yep.
Uh.
It says here that you don't got plans today.
I don't. Not for work, at any rate.
Call it a day off.
Holy , watch out, you might enjoy yourself or somethin'.
Oh, I plan on it.

A week already?
Damn.
Got your list for me?
Yeah.
Hey.
Thanks again.
'S fine.
Hey, I been wondering.
You a boy?
Uh.
No, prolly not.
Tomboy, then?
Ehhh, ish?
I used to say I was a girl who was really bad at bein' a girl.
Mhm.
But more and more, I think I'm not either, y'know?
Does that sound weird?
No, not really.
Okay.
Thanks.
When I was your age, I'd get people saying I was no good at being a man.
Oh. Why?
Jealousy, I bet, because I'm real good at being a man, ha.

Good enough to be a real man's man, y'know?
Like, what, you're gay?
Yeah.
Oh, okay.
Not exactly the same thing YOU got goin' on, but.
I'm still glad to know.
Izzat weird?
You work for a shadow deer feared throughout this green, humid hell.
Nothing is weird.
Good point.
Yeah.
"Good luck, kiddo."
Okay.
Mimi's
Here it goes.

Oh, hey.
Surprised to see you here.
Heh. Yeah. "Surprised."
Though I shouldn't be.
Given the company you keep.
Wait, what?
Ohhh no.
mhm.

Uh.
Hey.
Hello, Fawn.
Thought you were off today?
I am.
I'm here to enjoy myself.
And you? Done with your work already?
Yeah, uh, I just had some free time, you know?
Wonderful.
Well, why don't you join me?
Go get us some drinks.
My treat.
How the hell did you mess this up?
You think he knows?
...
He knows, huh.
Why hasn't he called me on it yet?
He tryin'a catch me?
Likely.
Why, though?
That man has one pleasure in life: cruelty.
He wants to see you squirm.

It's now or never. I won't get a second shot.
You're gonna have to distract him.
Excuse me?!?
Distract him.
SLAM
What the hell do you expect me to do, pull out a tit and slap him with it?
Fawn!
No, no, uh.
Definitely don't do that.
To him.
=sigh=
Fine.
In the next few days, I want the works. Chocolates. Cigars. If you find smut, bring it.
'Kay.
I'm about to get into a whole mess of trouble. You'll need to rescue me.
Those memories of yours better be worth it.

The Next Round's On Me, Everyone!

Woooooooo!

Woooo!

Yeah!!

Woooooo!

ooooo!

Just one catch, y'all! ♥

?!

You're gonna have to sing along. ♥

no

Woo!

Wooo!

Yeah!

Wooo!

SQUELCH
CLAP
CLAP
CLAP
mmhm
There we go, that's a good beat.
CLAP CLAP
CH CH CHCHK!
CLAP CLAP CLAP CLAP CLAP CL

?
Ohhhhhnnn a wanton heart
is an awful thing!
You want it quiet!
But it can't help but siiiiiiing!

If it's broken, then it's howlin'!
If it's in love, then it's yowlin'!
And sometimes it ain't worth the trouble it brings!
CLICK
That noise...
SSSSLIP

SINGING!
Ohhhhhh my wanton heart
fills me with DREAD.
Mimí

Mimi
LISten to HER!!!
Ooooooooh! I should've had her spayed when I had the chance!
If I don't keep an eye on her, she'll SWIPE the bar and the patrons' love from under me!
It lies in wait
like an old
warheaaaaaaad!!!
And you, you're still teasin' me!
You say there's no pleasin' me–
WHOA!
SLIP

Oooh when I get my hands on her-!
At least I had my outfit ready yyEEEEEE
=oof!=

So, take me home and I just might please you instead!
DROP
Aah!!!
Hooooly
That was. Just. Damn.
I sure am glad I got our drinks before all'a this SINGING started up suddenly!
Like, damn.
Lucky break right there.
End of Issue 7

The Hazards Of Love 8: Taking Leave

I. Am.
So so SO so so
very
very
VERY
Sorry.
I. Am.
AbsoLUTEly
mortified.
It's never
too late to
have them
spayed.
Ah ha ha,
of course.
But for now,
I'm interested
in a slightly less
expensive sort of
solution, you
understand!
A different
surgery.
Tongue?
No, no, she's
likely to still make
noise even without
the tongue.
Can we
remove her
voice?
I'd be
delighted.

Well, time to put your money where your mouth is, eh?
Juliana, I'm so sorry.
Heh.
I'm serious about the luxuries, you know. I get so few.
The chocolate, the cigars, the candies - and of course, don't forget the smut.
Granted, I'd rather you saved my voice.
But you must at least TRY to find the smut.
I'm so ' sorry.
=sigh=
Fawn.
Your poor arm!

Well, it won't heal any faster if you grab at it like that!
Why'd you haveta go so hard?!
You trust me too much.
Don't you DARE imply I trust you! I'm looking out for myself!
This was a cold and calculated move!
This is only opportunism on my part!
Thank you.
I won't let you down.
I'm gonna getchu that smut.
Haha!
Fawn.
We're leaving.

MERCADO GUSTAVO
ARREGLOS FUNERARIOS Y MUCHO MUCHO MAS
Hey.
Hey.
Welcome-
-back.
It didn't go well, did it?
I don't know.
Maybe it went okay?
I'll let you know if I survive.
You got my groceries?

I mean, I'm just waitin' for the other shoe to drop, like-
-oh, hold up, here he comes.
Why does this man have my groceries?
Just an exchange of favors; HI THERE, I'm Rafael Loya.
The kid promised an appointment with you if I took care of the groceries, and HERE WE ARE.
I'm just, uh, looking for a consultation?
Just a consultation.
I don't work for humans.

I know - I KNOW, but I've got the money!
I've GOT IT.
I can even pay you double.
Just. Please.
erámica "Isabel"
Fawn.
I didn't guarantee nothin'.
Good.
This will be settled immediately. Later, we'll have a conversation about this.
I won't have you owing debts.
Mr. Loya, I'm happy to provide you with a consultation at the rate you've offered.
Immediately.
...
Now?

Yes.
OKAY, so we're closin' early this fine day, got it.
Man, what the hell.
Don't worry about it, trust me.
I DO worry.
Well, then that's on you.
You have an hour.
What can I help you with?
I just – I have so many questions.
Mm.
How do you knit them?

You are aware that I'm a doctor, yes?
I don't need a doctor - I need someone who knows Bright World.
Someone who knows how to go from here to the human world, who can knit memories into a key.
O-or whatever it is you do.
I have been trying to talk to you for who knows how long-
And here you are, wasting our time on rumors.
Then TELL me!
I'm not asking you for information - just tell me what I've got wrong, if I've figured it out yet!
Why are you loyal to the others?! You're not like them! I see how they look at you, I hear what they say about you-
HAH
And what is it they say?

They don't know what you are.
They don't know when you arrived.
Mr. Loya, I believe we are finished here.
No!
If you leave now, you may keep all of your fingers.
No!
I've waited for SO LONG. You need to HELP ME.
This consultation is over.
You don't understand!
I'm doing this out of LOVE.
Really.
Tell me, then.
What is it you think you know of love?

Fawn, wait outside.

What?

WAIT OUTSIDE.

Damn, okay!

Damn.

Like. Damn.

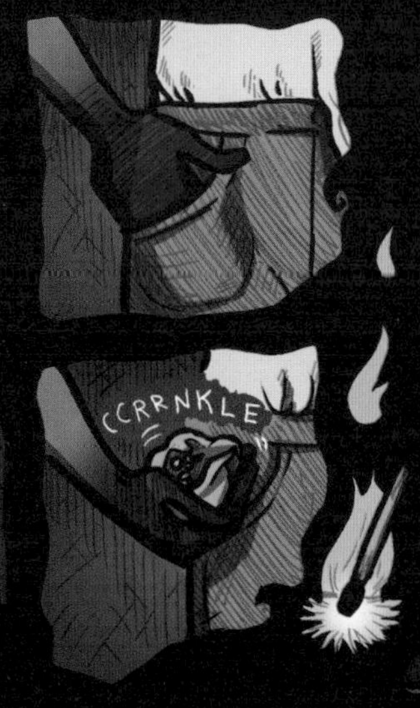

Abuela?
Where were you?
Oh. Oh, we gotta leave.
We gotta get out.
It took me so long to find you!
We're in a bad, bad place.
We gotta get back home-

oh
How long you been dead, Abue?
Oh, I can't tell.
Death makes time very different.
Oh.
Death brought me much clarity.
For example, the knowledge that your place in my life had been usurped!
That damned cat!
I couldn't rest until I found out what became of you... but first I had to find you! And I could not.
Until today.
You shone out in Bright World like a beacon!
Yeah, to hell with that cat.
That cat super tricked me and stole my name.

Yes. I'm given to understand that this happens.
WIPE
Can you get me home?
I'd give my life to get you home safely!
Unfortunately, I am already dead!
Abue.
You are in a lot of trouble, mi vida!
Humans can only leave Bright World if...
...they travel to
The Land of the DEAD.
...
But then you would be dead as well.
Yah, I guessed.
So this place - Bright World - is something different to the Land of the Dead?
From above, I see them all and I choose where I go. These places are side by side and on top of each other and also the same, depending which lens is used to view them.
...I'm sorry, that must not be very helpful. They, er, are a bit adjacent-
Oh!
SOB

THUD.
What was that?

Well, it definitely wasn't me.
And I definitely did not just drop the "fragile" box instead of gently laying it down.

Maybe if I-
Why are you this way?

Maybe it's time to take a break?
Oh, I see! Great idea.
CLINK

Yeah, I'm good at ideas.
Then you remember Pritha and Jay will be here in about a minute.

=Hissssssss= Buzzkill.
He's gotten better for a guy who used to think you were literally possessed by the devil.

...Hey.
Are we going to be okay?
Mrow?

You work nights at the bodega! All my classes are in the AM!
The distance between Brooklyn and Queens has ended many a relationship!
Pff.
Iolanthe.
I will bike from Jackson Heights to Crown Heights every damned day.
'S gonna be FINE.

Relax, okay?
WE are gonna be just fine.

I promise.
WIPE
Fawn.
FAWN.
I gotta go.

Hi, sorry, I'm here.
I'm here.
You've been crying.
...Yeah, I guess I was.
Nothing has happened to him that wasn't his own fault.

Remember that.
This is ALL his fault.
Escort him out.

If he tries to come back in, slit his throat.

2426

What HAPPENED?

What a thoughtful gift, fingers.
WHY.
Use them in good health, I guess?
Did you even have a plan?
Were you just tryin'a ■■■k me over, or what?
I'm helping US, you little ■■■stain; we're in this together! We're going to rip a hole in this ■■■n' HELL we're in, do you understand me?!
Let go!
Do you want him to find out?
Do you want to know what he'll do if he finds out what you were up to?
Let go.
LET GO!

HA HA HA HA Ohhh, Fawn! What a perfect Fawn, takes after him!
Shut up.
FAWN. You haven't figured it out yet, FAWN?
You think it's a coincidence he had "fawn" ready for you?
That I knew what your deal was?
Fawn isn't a name.
It's a TITLE.
You're not the first.
Odds are good you won't be the last.
End Of Issue 8

The Hazards Of Love 9: Where it HURTS

How many have there been?
Thirteen.
You're the fourteenth.
Why - why didn't you TELL me?!
You never asked me.
A better question for you to consider:
Why did he wait to tell you about the others until now?

Honestly, I'd made up my mind not to hire any more help.
It's never been worth the trouble.
What happened to the others?
Eventually, they all proved to be too delicate for the job.
Some opted to leave.
Some irritated me to the point where I refused to put up with them anymore.

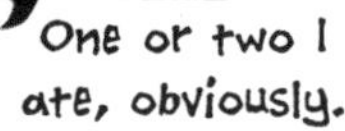

One or two I ate, obviously.
Obviously.
I hadn't planned on employing someone new.
"Fawn" was the name I had available to use, and so it was the name I granted you.
That simple.

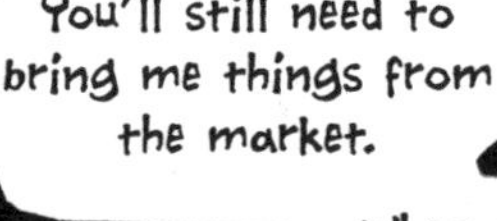

You'll still need to bring me things from the market.
When you do, keep in mind that the grocer is upset with both of us.
He sees you as an extention of myself; nothing more, really.
If he thinks it'd inconvenience me to damage you, he will.
Remember the cat, Fawn, and be wary of the grocer.

He wants to, like, blackmail me–
Regarding the earrings you stole?
You turned out to be quite the creative problem-solver after all, didn't you?
Clever with your hands, too, and more careful than I'd expected you to be.
Sit down.
You coulda just ASKED, is the thing.
Like.
"Fawn, you good at stealin' ?"
Oh, I suppose so.
Feel free to return the earrings, then.
Ask Mimi if you could have them, please.
No? Not interested in that option?
No, I thought not.

"Deserve." An interesting choice of word.
She made a choice. She caused an effect, sure as gravity.
And you feel that's UNFAIR.

She was helpin' me out!
Please. Just.
Don't hurt her because of that.
Fawn.
You care about her an awful lot, don't you?

Please WHAT, Fawn?
Please don't hurt her.
=sob=

Look at yourself. Look at how she's left you.
P-please
=sniff=
Like an open wound, a cut awaiting the sting of lime juice and salt.
=hiccup=
=sob=
So.

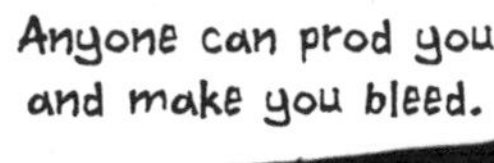
Anyone can prod you and make you bleed.

=sob=

We'll fix this.
Here is what will happen:

I won't perform the excision. She'll simply need to pretend I did.
This will be a secret. If my reputation suffers from it, I will chop her into small pieces and feed them to you.
I will do this for you, Fawn, ONCE. In return, you won't see Juliana again.
Is that clear?

No good can come from that one. She's filth.
This is for your own good.

Okay.
Okay.
Now, I WAS pleased with your skills.
It's why I'm enlisting you for a follow-up performance.
There is a minotaur. You will be stealing from it.
"You are well-armed, I've seen to that.
"The rest is up to your agility and ingenuity."
"How will I find it?"
"Finding it isn't the difficult part, Fawn.
"I'll drive you to its lair.

"It's taking the knife from its back that's the challenge.
"It craves flesh- what doesn't?- and if it sees you, it will devour you.
"But first it must see you.
"Be cunning.
"Be subtle.
?
Thlip Thlip Thlip
"But above all else...

"Be swift."

KRRK
please don't
please don't take it
Man, it's a literal ' knife in your literal ' back!
Don't it hurt?
yes, it hurts
but it's all i have left

Problem is, I'm gettin' the hang a how Bright World works.
If I let go a this knife, you turn around and eat me, right?
maybe?
i don't know
i lost everything that came before
i...
i can remember my ma
KRRK
i miss her
and i love her, i have that
i hope she is okay
i hope, i hope she loves me
Man–
will you hold me?
she used to hold me, but no one holds me anymore
Same.
It's gonna be okay, man.
Just–

I'm sorry.
CHHK

!
this!!!
that!!!

this awful ' surreal-ass ' place!!!
I miss MY mom, too!
What even is this?
It's hard to put into human terms, but I'll try.

It's a memory distilled into an object - well -
"memory" isn't quite nuanced enough.
It's a bit of mind, a bit of soul, a bit of time.
It's part of what makes creatures able to reason, crystallized into a tangible form.
This is very cleanly harvested, Fawn.
You should be extremely proud of yourself.
I feel sick.
Don't be so dramatic; it wasn't that bad.
It was bad.
My head hurts.
Mm.
You'll get used to it.

Pft, that sounds as stupid as you do.
EY!
Keep it down!
Oh, it's fine, Mimí's getting her beauty sleep.
No one can hear us.
What if she wakes up?
I left a mess of bottles outside her door. We'll hear the screams and breaking glass all the way down here.
Okay. Good.
You're gonna have to keep an eye out.
Since I can't risk looking at you.
God, you're so dramatic.
And can you PLEASE be nice to me? Things are rough and my head hurts.
Okay.
Okay.
Also I gotchu some smut.
SMUT!

"A hand mashed against the face of the other human.
"Fingers tangled in the inexplicable mass of longer, coarser hair that seems to only sprout on top of the skull.
Hot.
"A mouth was placed over the human's skin. It was very wet.
Whoa.
"The flesh was soft, succulent, rich with blood and flavor."
Yep, there it is. Gross. Why. Ugh.
It's starting to go gray. You should get going.
Yeah, I gotta have th' coffee ready before he gets up.
I don't even know.
If he even sleeps.
Is your head any better?
Nope.
But, uh.
That was, uh. Still real nice, anyways.
Hmp. Feel better soon.
Thanks.
...He's just torturing you.
You know that, right?

I thought he was tryin'a make me into a creepy shadowthing like him.
Maybe it's both.
He strikes me as a multi-tasker.
Think he was human? Him and Mimi and all the rest?
Not the Bright Worlders. But your guy...
...he HAS to be something else, the way everyone acts.
You think Bright World made him whatever he is? If he was a human?
Maybe?
I wouldn't be surprised.
There's a million ways Bright World destroys us.
Yeah, uh.
I think he made me kill someone?
Oh.
Oh, sweetie.
=sob=
I'm sorry, I'm so sorry.
Maybe that wasn't what happened?

No, your instincts are probably right.
Here. Keep your eyes shut.

I-I took a knife outta a minotaur's back and =sniff= they turned into a monster and they couldn't talk no more and I know it don't make sense =sob=

No, it doesn't.
But I believe you, anyway.

Thanks. That means a lot.
I'm not happy about it, so you know.

About what? Believing me?
Trusting you.

It's a trap.
Liking each other might get us killed.
Hope is deadly.

They'll use us to chip pieces off each other until there's nothing left.
Well, this ain't ending like that!

It's just you and me.
Tryin'a keep the damage to a minimum.

It's a nice thought, but you've got two goals.
You want to go home, remember?
This is my awful, awful, awful home.
Fine! So we add a "Juliana gets a better situation" to our goals! That easy!
Like, damn, there's no reason we can't aim high!
We're TEAM HUMAN!
... Think we got a shot?
Ha. No.
But let's try anyway.
End of Issue 9

The Hazards Of Love 10: Ecdysis

This isn't my life.
I stole it, and I'm very proud of how this came about.
Kittens collect secrets.
They're lovely toys.
Fun to bat around.
Chewy.
However, some secrets are better than others, and I found one worth keeping.
You can steal a human's skin and walk around wearing their shape and living their life.
Imagine! I was only a kitten at the time, but I knew this was special.
And so I kept this secret as I grew, and thought about it often. What I could have!
I could wear clothing and always be warm!
I could eat when I wanted, whatever I wanted!
I could go everywhere and learn everything!
Oh, I wanted it so!

And so, one day...
...I crossed into the Bright World to learn how it's done.
Bright World is not a kind place. It is not a safe place. But it had what I needed.
I lost many lives.
Some were drowned.
Some were ripped out of me.
And one I gave to the jaguar for her secrets.
My dear cousin, it's not their skin you steal!
It's their name.
Begin with a drop of their blood.

Their blood holds the secret to their shape.
Take a drop
Wrap it in their name
Swallow it down.
You will be granted their shape, and Bright World will claim the rest.
Thank you, cousin.
Have I done you a favor, cousin? I do not know.
Go and choose your shape with compassion.
I took her words to heart,
and I learned about right and wrong,
good and bad.
And ethical consumption.
This choice gave me a chance to bring happiness where there was none.
(Or so I'd thought.)
(If I knew then what I know now... well, I may have still made the same choice.
I don't know.)
It brought me people to love and be loved by, who I would NEVER hurt or harm (I thought).

Life, however, is complicated and brief.

All nine of our lives will not equal one human's.

And here I am, at the end of a life.

I am wiser. I am more contemplative. I have drunk deep of love.

Would the creature whose name I stole have done the same?

Would they have learned to love, to work, the way I did?

In particular, it is brief if you are a cat who wears a human shape.

They were a kitten, I know that now.

And I barely listened to them the night I sent them to their death.

Am I any better?

I will hurt my loved ones with my departure.

They will mourn for Amparo, who is long gone.

I have no time for laments.

My time is finished. What's done is done.

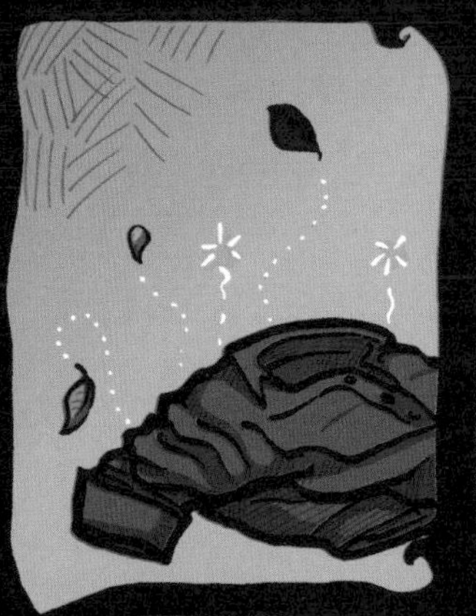

...But I think I made a mistake.

Amparo?
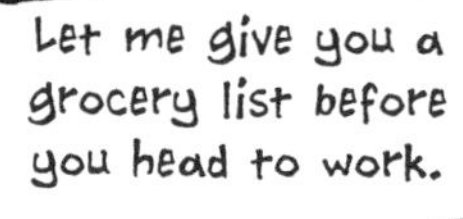
Let me give you a grocery list before you head to work.

ZIP!

We need-
...
Amparo?

Amparo?

What did you end up doing with the fingers, Fawn?

I ripped one off and threw it to distract the minotaur, and I guess he ate it? But, anyways I lost the other two during me getting the knife-

Oh, is that all?

I had wondered why you hadn't just taken them off, really.

Alright, time to put theory into practice.

If you're going to clean my Extraction Room, you'll need to get there.

Take a breath. You know where we're going.

Okay.

Ready? We're only going to step to the...

SIDE.

oh holy

There. Simple as-

HRNG!!

Blarg!

Disgusting.

Clean that up.

Hey. Uh.

I lost a tooth...?

Let me take a look.

Mm.

Well.

You're becoming an adult, I suppose.

I don't think it was the sidestep, but you're right. Your teeth are definitely a little loose.

Aww-uh-eh?

All of them, yes. Let's keep an eye on them.

If it gets worse, I'll splint them. How's your head doing?

SLURP

What does that taste like to you?

Uhhhhhh.

I dunno?

Kinda sweet, I guess.

Subject paused, slack-jawed for several seconds. They stated they did not know the answer to my question, then changed their mind but seem ... tice of their real

Why are you like this?

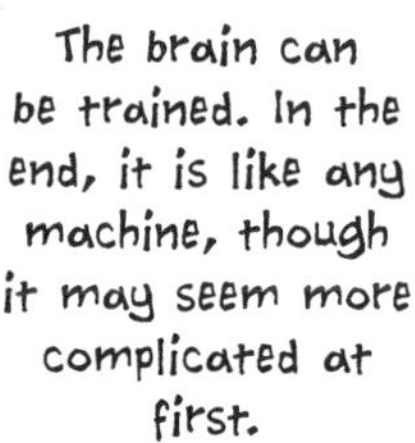
The brain can be trained. In the end, it is like any machine, though it may seem more complicated at first.
SNIP.
SNIP.
SNIP.
However, each part, each cog, each and every sensor has a function it provides.
Learn which button to press, which synapse to fire...
SNIP.
...and you can train yourself, coax your brain into functioning at its best.
The brain learns, changes, grows new pathways.
FZZZZM
One can wonderfully adapt to anything given enough time.
SCRAPE
SCRAPE
You ain't subtle.
What need have I for subtlety?

WHAT THE !!

WHAT THE !

Fawn, really.

Is all this swearing necessary?

PAP PIP PIP PAP PIP PIP PAP PAP PAP

You threw your teeth at me.
WHAT THE [scribbled out]K!!
Fawn. Calm down.
MY TEETH!
You're upset and unable to see the big picture.
IS IT A PICTURE OF THE BLOODY TEETH I SPAT UP?!
They've been replaced, Fawn.
I'd have thought you'd be pleased.
WIPE
Look at yourself.
A nascent predator.
Bright World seems to find ways of giving us what we really want.
UGH, he is SO full of it.

Maybe he's right.
You ain't all toothed out. Deformed.
Maybe Bright World knows how bad I am and it's makin' me into this.
~~BULLSHIT~~.
AH!
SLAM!
What's the worst thing you remember doing?
Uh. I got into fights a lot, and–
No, don't look at me.
Fights. And?
I...stole stuff from the CVS.
That's the worst, I guess.
Okay.
None of that is evil. It's not great, but it doesn't mean you're inherently, irrevocably wicked.
You don't know that.
I know you've got a lot of growing up to do! I know you're in an awful place! I know you've stuck your neck out for me since Day One, even when I told you I wouldn't do the same!
=sigh= Fawn, you don't deserve this.
But it's easier for him to hurt you if you think so.
Because he's a PILL.
Whoa, whoa.
Let's watch the ~~fuckin'~~ language.

Ah, sorry, that should be "he's a ~~fucking~~ pill."
Haha!
There ya go!
You don't secretly want what's happening to you; he's trying to brainwash you.
Promise.
I don't want what's happening to me, either.
If Bright World gave us what we wanted, I'd be sitting in a hot bubble bath, eating chocolates, drinking sparkles, smoking a cigar and fiddling with myself shamelessly.
oh boy
And if it knew my deepest secrets, what my heart aches for?
I'd have a job that used my mind, not my hands.
I want to learn things.
Even – maybe especially – here!
That's my secret. I want to know EVERYTHING.
I want to be a walking encyclopedia!
Well, damn, Juliana. You wanna know anything I can tell you, just ask.
Well. There is one thing.
Off the top of my head, anyway.
You can't make fun of me.
I swear.
If you do, I'll–
I'll throw my dishrag at you!
Ha, just ask!
Who is The CVS?

Mm. I'd like to see you looking less terrible.
Yeah, man, that makes two of us!
The fu—
Wait, this ain't gonna lead to, like, plastic surgery, right?
What could you do if it did?
Cry, I guess.
As much as I enjoy your anguish, I meant you need nicer clothes.
I'm sending you to The Seamstress.
Ey, I could hear capital letters in that. Sounds like she'll try to kill me.
Don't be a pessimist.
She could succeed.
Excuse me, human!
El Ciervo's Fawn asked me to deliver a message to you!
(And also some chocolates.)

What do you know about
"The Seemstress"

Also enjoy some chocolates

She sent you this.

Thank you, my good snail.

→ Doña Blanca
(use her name, b
polite)
→ Always hungry
(take snacks)
→ Cunning
→ Crafty
→ Be careful
→ Thanks, I guess :)

And who is this who darkens my door?

'Sup, I'm Fawn.
El Ciervo sent me to get a new outfit from you.
Ohhh, I see, I see!
I should've guessed!
You look like him.
Like El Ciervo?
Spitting image.
Did he send me a snack?
He sent you money, is what he sent!
Is thaaat whaaat he told you?
HA HA HA HA
Maybe you are the snack.
NOPE, nope, I got that handled.
stroke
'Sides. You don't wanna eat his assistant. He'd get all cranky.
Ohhh, little sweetmeat!
You can bluff better than that, can't you?

As if he didn't send me the occasional mouthful of venison.
Now!
Shall we weave a charming little suit for you?
Sure. Hey, um, by the way.
If you get hungry, I got more bones.
I know that, silly!
In my bag, I mean.
Ohhh.
A very important distinction.
You've been in Bright World for awhile then, haven't you?
Yes, ma'am!
Long enough to know time is messed up here, anyways.
Bah, time.
Keep that nonsense in the human world, thank you.
Y'all got time! The market opens and closes. The sky goes white.
Well, yes, some of us enjoy pretending time is relevant to our lives.
But at least we're creative about it.
None of this boring "static measurement" thing! We give it some variety, some flair!

How does that line up with the human world?
Ah, little sweet. I'll give you information...
...if you TRADE.
=ULP=
For the answer to that, I'll need an IMPORTANT, tasty bit of human.
=TUG=
Perhaps...
Your NAME.
I already lost that.
What?
=Sigh= Magic cat stole it, shoved me in here.
Well. Drat.
Yeah, I'm pretty ' displeased, too.
And of course he didn't tell me.
Let me make a fool of myself instead.
Sadistic scoundrel. I suppose any kind of pain pleases him.
Who, El Ciervo? Yeah, he's a piece of !
I hate him, too!
I've half a mind to send you back alive, just to teach him a lesson!
Good idea!
Hey, uh.
You ever send any a the others back to him?
A few, if I recall correctly.
Definitely Veronica.

She shone like light on a river, and I made her shoes that kept her feet delicately, beautifully en pointe.

Where is she now?

That's the question on everyone's mind, I think.

"Go home, little Fawn, and open your eyes."

"Uh. What?"

"No hay peor ciego que el que no quiere ver."

Oh, damn.

Why're my eyes closed?
Ah, she told you.
Am I asleep? Am I in a coma?
You're awake and you're here.
Holding your eyes closed is voluntary, Fawn.
Perhaps there is something you don't want to see.
Open your eyes, then.
Where's Veronica?
Veronica drowned herself.
And the others?
They all dead?
Open your eyes.
Open your eyes.
You kill 'em all?

There we are. Hello, Fawn.
Oh, no.
END OF ISSUE 10

The Hazards Of Love 11 : Ciervo y Cervato

Okay.
SSING
FEB 04
York City
Name:
Amparo Uribe
Age: 24
$REWARD
ck Hair
wn Eyes
www.whereisamparo.
Okay.
...
This is ~~bullshit~~.
But even if it IS ~~bullshit~~, it's ~~bullshit~~ designed to work whether or not I believe in it.
And whether or not I talk out loud to myself.
Like a fool.
oh boy
Okay.

Amparo Uribe!
Wherever you are, you WILL hear me. Wherever you are, you will long to return to me!
The path to me is your path home, a light in the distance!
By my breath
By my tears
By the fires of our love
By the land where you dwelled
Come BACK to me!
Please come back.
mew!!!
Oh, HECK!

PPPPUURRRRRRRRRRRRR
=PURR=
Amparo, if you died and got reincarnated into a cat, blink twice or something.
=PURR=
So.
Good news or bad news first?
Good.
Gives me something to hold onto when the bad news hits.

Iolanthe came home early.
Good? That's GREAT.
She needs at least ONE night a week where she's not out 'til 1 AM hanging up posters-
-wait, what's the bad news?
She got a cat.
WH
AND she made you an F.A.Q.
Iolanthe's Guide
Lease: I checked, cats are fine
Vet visit: done
Microchip: none (no owner :( )
Vaccines: administered
Worms: will be gone soon!
Extra work Pritha will need to do: ∅ !
Will the cat let you put her in baby clothes?
Maybe...
What a deal!
'Cause you both nerds.
How dare she use my love for lists against me.
Also, possibly, there's a small chance Amparo died and is reincarnated in this cat.
Very small.
Infinitesimal.
Miniscule.
I don't really believe it, but-
Iolanthe.

I know this isn't them.
Just.
I saw their mom today and she's so, so tired.
=prr=
Nobody's looking for them, the police aren't even trying, and something is WRONG.
I know it sounds like I'm the crazy girlfriend who got ditched, but they-
-they wouldn't have just LEFT.
Jason-
Yeah.
We can't get anyone to even ADMIT that Amparo might be in trouble!
Or... dead.
mow?
Jay, you KNOW they wouldn't have just left.
Yup.
I'd believe the cat thing first.
Fine, we're keeping the goblin-baby.
But it's gonna have to get used to wearing cute sweaters!
Christ, this place gives me the creeps.
You mean Gowanus?

You know what I mean. It gets creepy here at 2 AM.
Big Al must have nerves of steel.
Yeah, Al's hardcore. Surprised they don't have her on enforcement.
Eh, any old butch can swing a bat.
Al's got skills.
She a people person?
Oh?
Nah, she researches.
Give 'er a week and a target.
She'll get as much dirt as you stalkin' an ex's social media.
Rude.
Hi!
Excuse me!
Hi, can you help?
Yeah,
Still, I couldn't work here like she does.
What, nights?
"Nah."
Excuse me.
I need your help!
Hi!
Hello?
"Alone."
Okay, okay, all of you, shut up!

I'm seeing a lot of new, chatty faces tonight.
So, it's time to give The Speech again.
One: if I went out and dealt with all your final wishes
(Told Billy you love him and your secret treasure is buried in Newark or whatever)
I'd never get stuff done.
So, this leads to two:
You scratch my back, I scratch yours.
We are trying to bring down Edwin Bishop, slumlord and general piece of filth.
I got his office address here, and I got his home address here.
Haunt the hell out of him. Memorize his passwords, his schedule, anything we can use.
Bring me back some good stuff, and we'll talk.
This is ethically dubious.
Eh.
Take it or leave it, no skin off my nose.
Good luck outrunning La Flaca.
grumble grumble
grumble grumble
I can't believe I have homework; I'm DEAD.
grumble
Excuse me, er, miss?
Just "Al" is fine.
I have all the things you asked for.

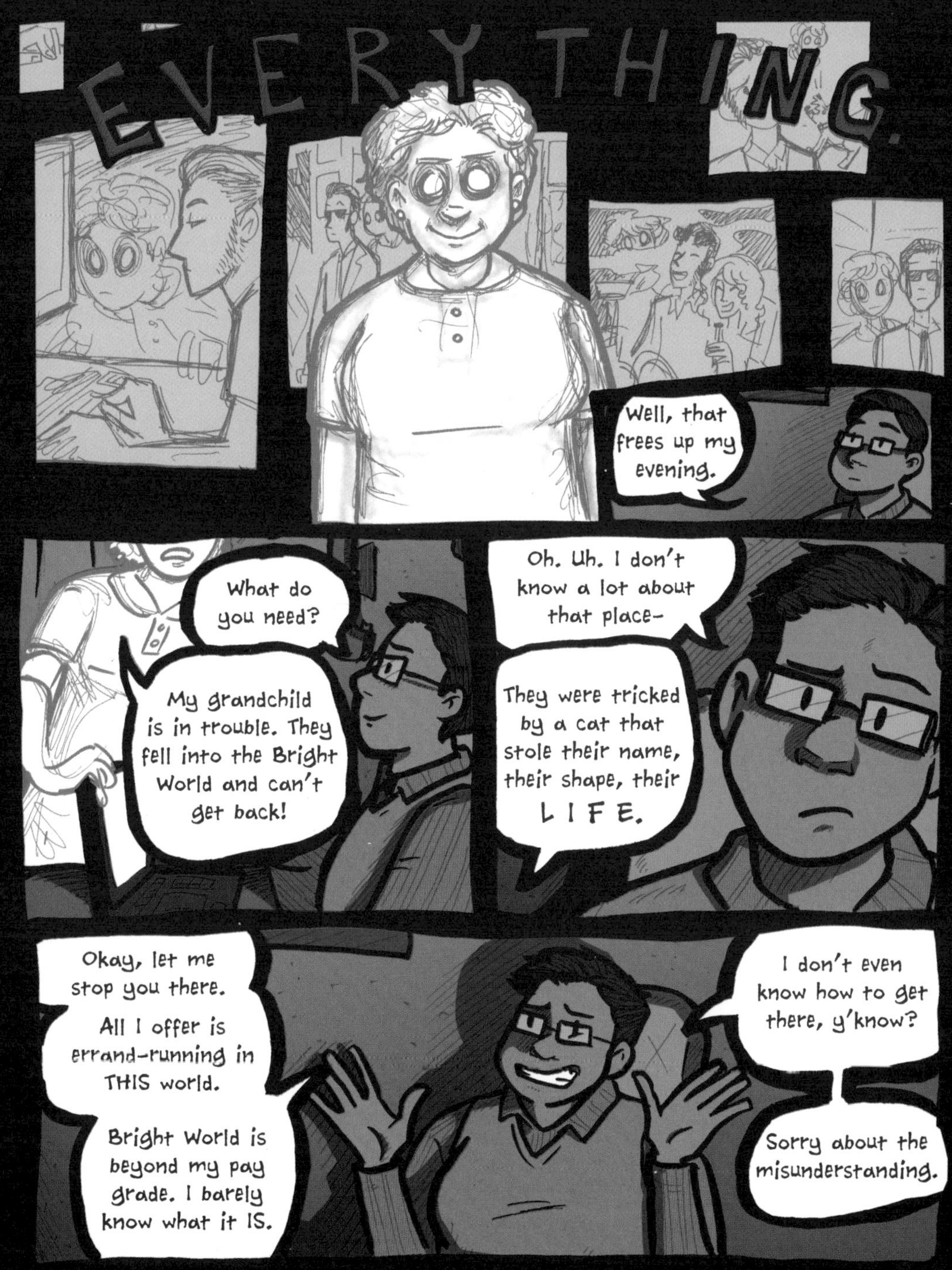
EVERYTHING.
Well, that frees up my evening.
What do you need?
My grandchild is in trouble. They fell into the Bright World and can't get back!
Oh. Uh. I don't know a lot about that place-
They were tricked by a cat that stole their name, their shape, their LIFE.
Okay, let me stop you there.
All I offer is errand-running in THIS world.
Bright World is beyond my pay grade. I barely know what it IS.
I don't even know how to get there, y'know?
Sorry about the misunderstanding.

"And there's no way I'm walking up to your son or whatever and, uh, I dunno,

telling them that their kid got replaced by a cat or whatever-"

Let's have an honest discussion, shall we?

Why are you doing this to me?

Doing what?
You grew those on your own.
On some level, you want what's happening to you.

No.
No, I... wanna go home.
I wanna go HOME.

It's impossible to get to the human world from here.
But let's say you managed, somehow.

Do you think your loved ones would recognize you as you are?
Do you think there's even anyone left who remembers who you are?

And even then, even then, when your feet touched that dim, desaturated earth... you'd corrupt it with every step you took, until you ripped a hole between there and here, and fell back in.
There's no return for you, Fawn.

You're lying.
Why would I lie?

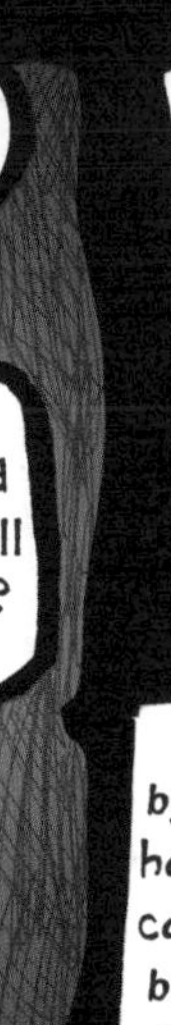

Three died by misadventure.

Their own fault, really.

Three died by their own hand, and I can hardly be blamed for that.

...You're missing one.

How come she ain't on your ███-up trophy wall then, huh?
Wipe the FILTH from your ears; the river swept her body away.
If you found all'a the others' corpses, you woulda looked for hers, too!
Instead you get all pissy anytime she comes up!
...
███, you think she got away.

WHM!
SLAM

I knew you were stupid, but I didn't think you'd be stupid enough to grasp at straws.
Such naïvety doesn't suit you, Fawn. Look at yourself.

You've never been naïve, never innocent. The word "child" never applied to you.
Born a liar. Born a predator.
You are exactly where a monster like you deserves to be.
You can say all that about me, and maybe it might even be true.

B-Rring
B-Rring
B-Rring

lo-lo, your phone.

Not me. Mine's in my pocket.

Burner phone?
It's the one I put on the posters!
Oh MAN, why didn't they just text?!
Hello?
Hello?!
Hi.
Uh.
Hi, I have information about Amparo.
...
Are...
Are you going to tell me, or...?
I mean, yeah, yeah. That's why I called. It's just, it's weird.
Can we talk in person?
Are they okay?
Yeah.
They're fine.
They are NOT fine!
It's really complicated.
You're aware this sounds so sketchy, right?
I'm SO aware, yes.
=sigh=
Ah, give me a quick second.
Okay, this must be Iolanthe. Yes?
...
Yes.
Okay.
Iolanthe. You were Amparo's girlfriend, Since... high school?

Amparo wore a, uh – a shiny purple suit to your graduation ceremony.
It had violet glitter lapels.
Yeah, there was a trail of glitter all through their mom's apartment. Jeez.
You helped clean it up, and when you were done, their abuela fed you pork and chile tamales.
...You still there?
Yeah, I'm here.
Can we please meet at, like, a diner or some place publicish?
Yeah.
Yeah, let's do that.
I really must congratulate you, Fawn.
I let down my guard.
You found a weak spot, you struck.
It proves my point.
To be honest, I'm delighted I decided to keep you.
Awful little creature.
You're alert, you adapt quickly, and you learned to use your hands.
I never would have sought you out, but like a parasite, you found someone to benefit from.
And you're learning.

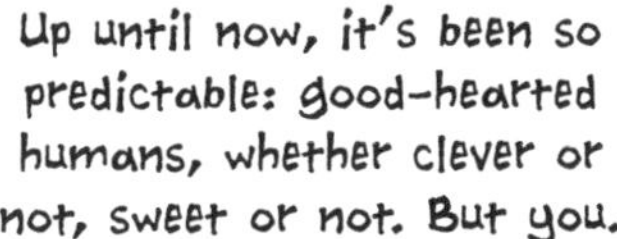
Up until now, it's been so predictable: good-hearted humans, whether clever or not, sweet or not. But you.
Who could mistake you for a good person?

Much less as noble or pure of heart.
Even now, you find ways to surprise.
Everything I'm saying, you're thinking how to use it to your advantage.

Look at you shake.
I bet you'd like to kill me.
I took you in as a novelty.
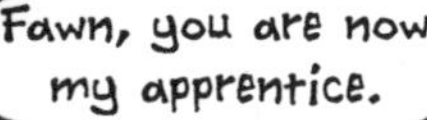
Fawn, you are now my apprentice.
Your attempts to do so will be very educational for you and extremely enjoyable for me.
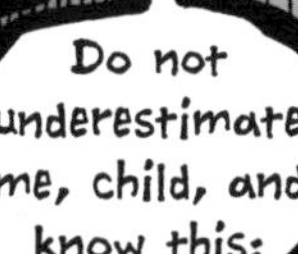
You'll receive a small stipend and much more freedom.
Do not underestimate me, child, and know this:
I will not underestimate YOU.

Buenas tardes.

Bienvenida.

Mas, que sorpresa verla de visita aquí.

No vine a verte a ti, alimaña.

Mirate nomas, cervato.

Y yo pidiendo tu ayuda.

Uh. Sure?

We'll talk in private.

SLAM

Okay, so I don't know you, but, uh.

Hi, I'm in trouble, please help me?

Eitale, eitale.

Relax.

Let me light my cigar first.

YIP

Fwooooo
HUFFF
I don't think you'd want my help, anyway.
Not yet.
I'm here because you can help me.
A ghost came through here some time ago, looking for you, yes?
That's all she had permission to do.
Where is she now?
I'm not gonna narc on my abue.
Damn.
Heh.
Slowing me down makes it worse for her, cervato.
Right now, I find her, I take her back to the shore, I leave her where she needs to be.
It's fine.
But if she makes me chase her longer, well.
I'll get tired.
I'll let her go.
She'll wander around, fading more and more. She'll forget what she was doing.
She'll forget where she needs to go, how to get there.
Eventually, she'll forget who she is.

Nothing more than a restless spirit.
A terrible fate for any of the dead.
AROO
You're Death then.
I told you my help wasn't what you wanted.
WAG WAG
But you wouldn't be the first Fawn to seek me out.
Was one of 'em Veronica?
Ha ha ha!
No, cervato.
She passed by my shores but never set foot on them.
Don't tell HIM that. Let him wonder.
What a good question you ask!
And oh, how helpful I am, eh?
Abuela wanted to help me.
I don't know where she'd go to make that happen.
Well. She'll need a medium, so I'll start there.

Ey.
No hay mal que dure cien años...
Ruffle
Ruffle
Ni cuerpo que lo resista.
Cuidate.
Fuera de mi camino, inútil.
God.
Did she smoke in here?
It reeks.
She really don't like you, huh?
Mm.

POSEIDON DINER IV
You're Al?
Yup.
Iolanthe, I presume.
Please sit, grab a coffee. This is gonna get pretty strange.
Are they alive?
Yeah, last I heard.
But they're in a lot of trouble.
Well.
That's a start, at least.
Where's Amparo?
END OF ISSUE 11 AND ARC ONE

Stan Stanley makes comics that are sometimes creepy, sometimes funny, but always queer. She's been making comics since she was in high school and has continued doing so throughout various science-related careers when she was supposed to be doing science. Instead, she created *Friendly Hostility*, *The Hazards of Love*, and her online journal comic, *Stananigans*. *The Hazards of Love* is heavily influenced by the ephemera of the Mexico in which Stan grew up, though she now finds herself in NYC among a lovely crew of weirdos. She lives with her spouse, a large cat, and a larger collection of bones.

A lot of people deserve thanks for this book. So, thank you:

TO MY EDITORS, Hazel Newlevant and Amanda Meadows. I learned so much from you; getting this book looking this polished wouldn't have happened without your keen editorial eyes and guidance as I learned how to digitally color.

TO MY MOM, who taught me that the 1998 *Godzilla* film is actually the bittersweet story of a single mom immigrating to the U.S. to find a better home for her kids, and if you squint at the end credits, she manages to do exactly that. Death of the author indeed.

TO MY TIA TERE, my other mother, who doesn't want to date or marry anyone of any gender, but does love her family pretty ferociously and always had gum in her pocket for me.

TO MY TIA LUPE, my other other mother, and to my Tia Moni, my other other oth- maybe I should just say thank you to my family as a whole. Thank you. I know I was often bewildering and strange, but you loved me anyway.

TO MARINA T., beautiful and smart and much more socially adept than I'll ever be. I miss you, I love you, I get nostalgic for pajama days and midnight pancakes.

TO ALIZA N., a sheer force of nature who happens to be incredibly kind, incredibly sweet, and absolutely lovely in all ways. I'm so lucky you're in my life.

TO ABBY E., who loves insects and skulls and science and comics as much as I do. I don't know where you were when I was 5, but what matters is you're here now and we can have sushi and talk about our favorite moths.

TO JACK AND ZELMA AND ARI, dear friends who I carry in my heart as though they were surgically placed there by a less-than-ethical deermonster doctor. Thank you for discussions on narrative framing and general cheerleading.

TO EVERYONE who has been reading my work since I was an awkward teen posting badly-scanned pencil drawings online. I appreciate you so much and I hope you've liked seeing my work grow and change. Thanks for sticking it out.

And most of all, TO ILAN N., who is shockingly good at that whole "true love" thing. This book wouldn't exist without you.

Hiya. Thanks for reading this comic!

If you liked *The Hazards of Love*, you might want to look into some of the people and films that influenced its creation:

Historical Figures

- Chavela Vargas
- Amelio Robles Ávila
- Sor Juana Inés de la Cruz and her patron, the Countess she called 'Divina Lysi'

Artists

- Leonor Fini
- Remedios Varo
- Kati Horna
- Leonora Carrington

Films

- *El Libro de Piedra* (1969)
- *Hasta el Viento Tiene Miedo* (1968)
- *El Vampiro* (1957)
- *La Maldición de la Llorona* (1961)
- *El Espejo de la Bruja* (1962)

(They're old, and the special effects are really cheesy, but the stories can be surprisingly good, and their creepy ambiance directly influenced this comic.)